P9-CCE-117

CONTENTS

religion professionals. The pastor's or rabbi's role.
How clergy live.

OPPORTUNITIES

in

Religious Service Careers

REVISED EDITION

JOHN OLIVER NELSON

VGM Career Books

Chicago   New York   San Francisco   Lisbon   London   Madrid   Mexico City
Milan   New Delhi   San Juan   Seoul   Singapore   Sydney   Toronto

Library of Congress Cataloging-in-Publication Data

Nelson, John Oliver.
   Opportunities in religious service careers / John Oliver Nelson. — Rev. ed.
      p.   cm.
   ISBN 0-07-141166-6
   1. Church work—Vocational guidance.   I. Title.

   BV683.N39   2003
   230'.0023—dc21   2003049719

1 2 3 4 5 6 7 8 9 0   LBM/LBM   2 1 0 9 8 7 6 5 4 3

ISBN 0-07-141166-6

Interior design by Rattray Design

This book is printed on acid-free paper.

FOREWORD

EVERY SUNDAY MILLIONS of people throughout the United States and Canada file into churches and cathedrals to worship. On other days, believers from among the wide variety of faiths represented in North America fill synagogues, mosques, and other houses of worship. Whether they are Protestants, Orthodox Christians, Catholics, Jews, Muslims, Buddhists, or adherents of other faiths, these people make religious worship an important part of their lives.

For some people, religion is not only a matter of belief but also the foundation for a career. Ministers, priests, rabbis, and other professionals earn their livings by providing religious services. The same is true of teachers of religion, pastoral counselors, ministers of music, and a variety of others employed by religious organizations.

There is one important difference between careers in religion and careers in most other fields: men and women who work in the area of religion tend to pursue their jobs out of a personal calling or conviction. Their main incentive is spiritual, not material. Their focus is on service, not the salaries or fringe benefits they earn.

Although they have the same basic needs as workers in other fields, professionals in this area follow their careers as a way of following God.

The material in this book is designed for those who feel some attraction to a religious service career. Perhaps you are one of these people. Maybe you have not made a commitment to any career, religious or otherwise, and are searching for your path. Or perhaps you are already working in a different career area, but wonder what it might be like to follow a religious profession.

In any case, you should benefit from the information provided here. From a historical background to an inside look at what it's really like to work as a professional religious leader, *Opportunities in Religious Services Careers* provides basic knowledge to help in your career planning. If you are considering religious service, be sure to take a close look at this information as you make important educational and occupational decisions. After all, your ability to serve others will depend on the quality and appropriateness of your own preparation. So here's wishing you the best, as you look at possibilities for a career in religious service.

Robert Edgar
General Secretary
National Council of Churches
New York, NY

1

THE NATURE OF RELIGIOUS CAREERS

WHEN YOU'RE IN emotional turmoil, where do you turn? Surveys indicate that most people in need first show up for help at the doorway of a minister, priest, rabbi, or other religious professional. These counselors frequently get the first chance, and often dozens more, to offer a hand to someone in need. Every day, men and women seek out a religious adviser they trust to help them through difficult times.

Sometimes this is so because these counselors are physically nearby. A steeple or a mission or a temple, with a side door unlocked and often someone waiting inside, is never far away. Then, too, a religious interviewer is inexpensive; somehow a congregation pays him or her to fulfill this role. Over the door are often the words "Enter, rest, pray," with no mention of an entry fee. Also, the helper here is almost always trained, whether in seminary or graduate school or through experience, to counsel.

Beyond these plain reasons—of being available, inexpensive, and trained—most of us seek out the religious adviser because he or she is spiritually concerned. When people stop in at that office, they expect to be taken seriously and not treated like just a "case" with a number. Not only today's problem ("crisis counseling"), but a whole life situation may need to be dealt with. And when in need, no matter how nonreligious or worried a person may be, it is good to be regarded as someone who is of concern to God.

The reason why Americans go, and even line up to talk to a religious leader, is not all clear. Does it date back to the time when the clergyperson was the one "authority" in town? Outside observers often marvel at how many Americans still go to church. One visitor remarked, "There's not that much exciting about the preaching, or the music, or the friendliness, or the sacraments—but they go!" Americans expect something greater from religion.

A Tough Job

Service as a professional religious helper may occur from behind a desk or on a park bench or in the street. Regardless of the setting, it is a demanding role. If the answers are too easy, the person being helped will soon realize the counselor has little to offer. Even creative listening is better than a glib response. Then, too, clergy are often approached for sympathy, food, or a little money.

Once found to be effective, the trained religious worker may often gain, by community grapevine, an insistent set of clients. The Sunday sermon or group meetings during the week are probably adequate for most members of a congregation, but there are many who need personal help again and again. Clergy are sometimes the only figures in the entire neighborhood who will ask to hear the whole story, who will seriously try to grapple with the individual's problem, and who will not gossip about it all over town.

Being the person for problems in a given community frequently demands being more than just a counselor, particularly in America. Often members of the clergy become the errand runners of the region and are asked to drive a neighbor to the clinic, look for the teenager who's playing hooky, help with a loan, say grace at a club luncheon, or sit on a porch rocker beside a senior citizen. Each of these chores provides a needed service, but it must be admitted that together such activities can be distracting and are really only of limited benefit to the community as a whole.

Why mention these pitfalls, which are common to many—though of course not all—careers in religion? It is to show how urgently workers in this field need to have their own deep resources and directives. Consider, for example, what the great Jane Addams, renowned social worker at Hull House in Chicago, told the author when she was very old. She said that for most of her life she had been against religion, churches, and synagogues, but had in later years changed her attitude. She began to realize that in decades of dealing with many social workers, she had found that a large proportion of them stayed at their jobs for only two or two and a half years and then quit. Typical, she said, was the young woman with graduate social work training who came in to resign: "Why should I wear myself out on these unresponsive, frustrating cases? People won't change! They leave me exhausted, day after day. Now I'm shifting to a job as a wholesale buyer at Marshall Field's." By contrast, Ms. Addams said she had grown to understand that those workers who had religious motivation somehow went on for many years, often growing in effectiveness. "Do they take home their problems and pray? Are they renewed by weekly worship to go back to it all? I don't really know," she said. "But I do know that nowadays I greatly prefer that anybody handling human need be upheld by a faith in God."

The picture is clear. Those who are earnest about helping people need a faith in life far higher and more profound than those involved in other kinds of daily work. For such a demanding role, nothing less than a "calling" will do.

The Helping Dimension

In our own time, either seeing events and problems in the larger perspective of ministering to others or with your faith in mind provides a real resource for being helpful to others. It means you can lend assistance by saying not, "Here are my ideas about what you should be doing," but rather, "Here is the broadest pattern of divine intention, into which you are called to fit your life." Thus you are not just doing somebody good, but suggesting where that person fits into an important story.

In fact, the do-gooder (an old, rather derisive term) is usually an unwelcome member of society. The famed cynic H. L. Mencken, early in the twentieth century, said something like, "If I find someone coming toward me to do me good, I get away as fast as I can!" Trying to manipulate people into some model of your own is a decidedly dubious venture and an almost always unhelpful one. But to convey a large religious vision in a scenario where each is at liberty to find his or her part is for many the most creative and redeeming work possible.

What has just been said might seem to imply that a sense of calling is a black-and-white, unmistakable set of signals. Most often it is anything but this! Rather it is a gradual or mysterious process. In the classic seventeenth-century book *Pilgrim's Progress*, which has been read by millions, as the potential pilgrim peers across a misty field, his guide asks, "Do you see yon gate?" Pilgrim knits his brow and answers, "No." The questioner says, "Then do you see the light above the gate?" The man strains his eyes and replies, "I think I see a light." Thereupon the adviser bids him to get going—to go toward the light, that dim clue. Often it is only such a half-hidden glimmer that any of us can ourselves follow, or commend to anybody else seeking help and direction.

In the next chapter we will look more closely at what having a calling can mean in the modern world. Thus far, we have briefly suggested that helping people is the beginning point of most careers in religion, and that if you are to devote yourself to this profession, you need a genuine call to it, an awareness that God deals directly with you and, through you, with others.

2

RESPONDING TO THE CALL

MANY PEOPLE FIND the whole concept of a call to service or a divine vocation mysterious and perplexing, even embarrassing. They ask, "Does it involve angels? Does it have to be like the boy Samuel hearing a voice in the night? Is there a heavenly hand laid upon one's shoulder?" Whatever the experience, critics tend to agree that it is a sort of vocational guidance available only to those who will go into employed religious work, and no others need apply. This sort of reasoning is a serious mistake.

What follows here is not an effort to convert anyone to any specific religion, proclaim an ultimate truth, or point out the infallibility of certain religious arguments and claims. Rather, it harkens back to where the whole meaning and power of calling in our own inherited culture originated. Without tracing the history of that idea, we are at a loss to understand vocation, calling, or the basis of the current American realization of work itself.

If your background is Jewish, Catholic, or Protestant, then you are part of the heritage we must briefly examine because these faiths make up the majority of religious service careers in the United States and Canada. If, on the other hand, your religious roots are elsewhere—Islam, Hinduism, Buddhism, Confucianism, Taoism, or another world faith—you should follow this quick study as an account of how American Christian or Jewish vocation progressed to where it is today, keeping in mind that some aspects may be applicable to you and your religious vocation.

Views About God

The Hebrew experience of God in person-to-person terms has been unique among religions. In contrast, religious systems of the Far East hold that the less personal we become, the more we are merged with the Deity. It is unreal to these believers to say that God could engage in actual dialogue with persons.

Is this a particularly crucial difference? Decades ago, an international Western assembly of scientists weighed the proposition that, if one question in all reality could be answered in terms of infallibility, what would it be? One speaker posed the query about how many galaxies there are. Another brought up quantum theory. Finally someone offered this as the crucial query beyond all others: is the universe friendly at heart? The assembly, hushed, agreed.

A popular definition of religion is that it's "betting your life there's a God," a sort of hazarded intuition upon which much of Western culture is based. To be sure, millions of us actually deny, in practice, that God does exist or that He is concerned with individuals on earth. Polls have found that over 90 percent of Americans believe in God—but partly because words such as "atheist" are quite unpopular. Most of us stop right there, unwilling to say anything about this Deity. The "In God We Trust" on United States coins becomes for most of us just a quaint motto.

In the Hebrew-Christian branch of humanity, do we really believe that every woman, man, and child on earth exists to fulfill a divine purpose? As we are all given scientific explanations for natural phenomena and human behavior, is it possible to believe that a Deity actually has an intention and a vocation for each of us?

Obviously any candidate for a career in religion must take seriously such questions inherited from our cultural past. This study doesn't require a formalized theology or creed. But it does involve answering the broadest questions about the existence and nature of the God we inherit through our tradition. Look at the four specific alternatives we face, each with its technical name:

1. You can be an *atheist*, convinced that there is no such thing as God anywhere. This view sometimes seems to trade divine omniscience for one's own; for example, "I've investigated all, and find not a trace . . ."

2. You can be a *deist*, allowing that, to judge by the reason and structure of things, a Deity seems to have existed at some time but is now remote from us and uninvolved with human beings. One university professor has claimed that the great majority of her colleagues are deists.

3. You can be an *agnostic* (from Greek roots meaning, "I do not know"). Here you merely assert that since supernatural questions have no dependable answers, it is better to give up any such big inquiries with a humble, "Sorry, I can't say." Thousands of scientists, but by no means all, share this don't-know attitude about a God.

4. You may say that you are a *theist*. This means in your mind and spirit you have a direct, mysterious relationship with a God who is (in our limited terms) personal.

Among these four choices (and probably all of us have moods of all four kinds) it is theists who find their place in the stream of spiritual awareness, seeking to trace, wonderingly, a purpose in the universe. It is they who find a deity taking part in human history and perhaps even carrying on a conversation with people like us.

A rabbi in the classic Broadway musical *Fiddler on the Roof* is shown actually bantering and bargaining with God. This is a modern echo of Old Testament leaders and Psalm writers who similarly conversed with Yahweh, and of New Testament figures who got their very words from the God freshly known through Jesus in Palestine. So it is in this succession of theists, and nowhere else, that personal vocation and a call of God are known. Always these are linked with belief and prayer and with events recounted in the Bible.

Can the candidate for a career in religion today know something of that awareness of God that the theist declares? Without a sense that your calling is linked to a higher purpose beyond monetary rewards, the helpfulness described in the first chapter is likely to run dry. Being called would be an illusion for the atheist. It is unlikely for the deist, and it is a dubious venture for the agnostic. Possibly it is only the dimmest "I think I see a light" motivation for even the theist. But as one of mankind's most vivid and historically revolutionary experiences, a spiritual vocation is worth striving for at any awareness level a candidate may have.

The Origins of Vocation

The general public often assumes that anybody having the experience of divine calling should hurry off to a seminary and plan to be ordained. If it is a genuine call, observers say, the recipient will surely sooner or later have to become a religious professional. Yet there is plenty of evidence all through history of people who, though very sure of their spiritual beliefs, knew that their work rested in living a layperson's life.

For those who respond to the calling to help others by way of their faith, it's often a result of a very personal call. The Hebrew word for call is *qahal*, which means not only "a summons," but "an assembly," "a gathering," and "a fellowship."

It is useful to point out that at no other time in human history has there been such a tradition of divine intervention or of personal trust in the Deity. Those who today realize (either vividly or vaguely) that they are being called by God, march in a fantastically lively, varied *qahal*. As a professor at Yale used to warn: "When it's Almighty God who says to you, 'Get thee up quickly!'—man or woman, you'd better get up quickly!"

In the fourth century A.D., a vocation or calling was an experience no layperson had. It had become a status conferred by a bishop to make someone a clergyperson, a monk, or a nun. This belief continued through the Middle Ages. Ordained people had a vocation, while all others found their life work only by heredity or by chance.

Is not this attitude exactly what we find today, among old and young, Catholic, Protestant, and Jew? Vocation has lost almost completely its connection with God, except in specialized Catholic usage. Today it is the term applied to all jobs and occupations, be they in the health care field or in teaching, business, or some other profession. Surrounded with such popular assumptions about vocation, anyone interested in a career in religion often is not aware that the idea came from the Judeo-Christian religious experience of being called by God to perform work.

The Heritage of Success

Alongside vocation as a holy concern for all believers, another current of history colors our occupational decisions today. This is our heritage of success as the goal and ideal of life work.

The idea of success stems from the fifteenth and sixteenth centuries, when there suddenly arose the almost global movement called the Protestant Reformation (together with the Roman Catholic Counter-Reformation that it soon summoned forth). The Protestant Reformation began when the German Augustinian monk Martin Luther stumbled upon a vocational truth that was quickly taken up by many thousands of believers. His rediscovery was that the Biblical New Testament meaning of the word *repent* called not merely for penance (as was then taught), but rather for an individual's about-face in answer to God. It was not because of Church ceremonies, he claimed, but because of each believer's faith and obedience that he or she was made right with the Creator. He preached that all persons could be witnesses, that "everyone can become Christ to one's neighbor." Echoing Jesus' teaching, Luther proclaimed that every occupation or place in life was equally holy if offered in obedience to God.

This assertion of every person's equality came during the same decades as other social, economic, and political developments. It gave Christian men and women fresh courage for daily work. Specifically, it assured them that the God they worshipped recognized no elite class and was as much concerned with their duties as with those of the clergy and other religious professionals. A second influential Reformation leader, John Calvin, announced that based on the Bible, every person's work was a manner of praising God, particularly if that work was well done. He went beyond that, in fact, and beyond Luther, to say that some occupations themselves were apparently "more splendid" than others in God's sight.

It was like a bombshell! Here at the threshold of the modern world were shouted the keynotes of Western European history: the priesthood of all believers, the importance of working hard, and even a spiritual grading of jobs. It is out of this sixteenth-century interpretation of calling and vocation that the European, capitalistic idea of work comes to us. What's more, it's not just work that is the inherited tradition, but work with the intention to succeed.

In line with these claims, the life goal of countless millions of men and women in countries influenced by Western culture has been to succeed in these terms. This motivating purpose, for good or ill, is found mainly in the world where Western capitalism has taken it; for it came directly out of Reformation Protestantism, which originally put it all very simply by saying, "To succeed is to live out God's intention for my life."

How widespread was this success motivation? Possibly even at its most demanding it was never known to most of the working population. But it was very real to leaders and to the rapidly growing middle class. Set against the stern discipline of the old monastic life, the new devotion to daily work has been called "Protestant asceticism." This principle particularly governed Germany and Great Britain. The Puritans fleeing England through Holland found, on their way to America, reinforcement among their Dutch Protestant brothers and sisters. The mindset of the settlers of New England, America's "founding fathers," and of the eighteenth-century Presbyterian immigrants who flooded our land, was prevailingly Calvinist and capitalist.

A nonbeliever in those times is said to have marveled, "I'd rather meet coming against me a regiment with drawn swords, than meet one Calvinist who believes he's doing the will of God!" Here we have the origins of success in our history. The idea has ruined many a career, even as it has amassed fortunes and built empires. These people worked hard, steadily tried to advance themselves, and moved up to better jobs because their forebears had done this to please God and fulfill his plan. Long after most of them had forgotten entirely what success was, they went on spending their lives seeking success! On a college campus a reporter asked a successful industrial executive who had just spoken there for his definition of success. He thought for a moment and said, "Sorry, I've been so busy succeeding, I've never really had time to sit down and ask what that all means."

Can we ourselves define success? It is not merely making a lot of money (though many might find that definition good enough). It is not receiving a great deal of recognition or being popular. In fact, success means so many things to so many different people that it does evade any specific definition. Nonetheless, striving for success, whatever that may be for the individual, is such a prevalent motivation in choosing one career over another that it demands our attention here as we ask the question: Can careers in religion ever reclaim the dignity and sense of purpose they once had?

Following a Calling

Just out of school and looking for a job, most young Americans take what they can get. They settle for an occupation that pays, whether or not it satisfies ambitions and special aptitudes. It is sometimes said that all it takes to find one's calling is to see a need (or a want ad) and realize that one has the ability to meet it. Unfortunately, such employment simplicity gets lost in the complications of supply and demand, with society itself making most of the decisions. For example, in one small college, 85 percent of the freshmen listed their first job preference as medicine, whereas not more than 2 percent could ever achieve this goal.

Be sure to recognize the process by which any of us finds a calling. Often as we look back at a whole career, it turns out that the really pivotal decisions were not those made with intense worry and consultation, but were the result of rather spur-of-the-moment, casual happenings that just came along. "I met this stranger at the corner, who said he'd just come from a job interview he'd turned down. I went over, got the job, and have been working my way up in it for thirty years." What openings do you see? What abilities and interests do you carry around with you? Consider some instances of how the real operation of calling (in many cases, divine calling) takes place:

- A student takes a high school bus trip through a city's most impoverished neighborhoods; then, troubled but exalted, the student accepts the challenge of helping the poor as his or her life's work.
- When his father dies unexpectedly, a recent college graduate with a business major finds how shoddy and seamy the family business is; he changes his plan of becoming a missionary and vows to reshape the family's business concerns.
- Rocked by a friend's death from AIDS, a young woman shifts her studies from journalism to virus research.
- A manufacturer with a large income stumbles upon the fact that nearby forests and rivers are a sacred trust; he forms a foundation to conserve and improve "the good earth" and becomes a major proponent of solar energy research.

- A customer service agent on the same floor with three hundred other employees decides quietly to raise the idealism of her coworkers and make office parties less tasteless; her tact and dedication have changed the whole atmosphere of the office.
- After seminary training, a young priest-to-be decides that he can better handle a shelter for runaway youth before he is ordained; responding to that imperative, he turns his attention to coordinating the program.
- A grocery clerk decides to make a small ministry out of his store job and is friendly, helpful, and concerned with customers; he also organizes an annual canned-food drive and participates actively in other community-sponsored programs for the needy.

Each of these is an example of a person who has seen a need and found the inner ability to meet it. All persons, regardless of faith, would do well to recognize and honor such callings and to trace in them the *qahal* or *klesis* that means that these people wish to serve others and satisfy their spiritual souls while performing their daily work.

The old phrase "full-time religious work," describing professional careers, is a misnomer. None of us is called to mere part-time service in a religious vocation. Preferable are such terms as "professional religious work," or "church-related occupations," or "temple-related professions." This gives an honored place to those whose motive is religious, and who regard their work as actually done in God's own sight. They may even find their most significant work done outside their paid job—in community chores, at home, or in group avocations. To help these persons see their activities in a total perspective is an important responsibility of the clergy.

Volunteer work may also prevent men and women from making an idol of their job or from becoming workaholics. When people discover what is often called intentional living, they realize that both paid work and volunteer work take their places in a broad, person-serving interpretation of what human life is all about. In this sense, many women and men today have dimensions in their lives and work that can be lifted up into a realization that all of us are indeed called by a higher power in the working out of our careers.

Knowing Your World and Yourself

In some quarters, it would seem that vocational guidance is merely the twofold process of obtaining test scores of ability and interest and then comparing these scores against a large list of available occupations. Such procedures ignore some of the crucial factors in significant job choice: What do I think needs to be done in society (whether there is an occupation in that spot or not)? What changes of mood and intention can I, or others, foretell in my own matur-ing self? What, if any, is my overall purpose in living?

To deal with some of these queries, you will need to delve fur-ther into the choice of any life work and the best ways of sizing up the whole occupational field:

• **Know yourself.** Consider taking all the tests you can find of interest, aptitude, and personality at a school or guidance center or through online sources. Try your hand at summer jobs. Look at what your school experiences have told you: Do you lead in your group, or follow? Do you communicate well with words and atti-tudes, or are you often misunderstood? Are you more likely to be chosen as chairperson, recording secretary, treasurer, or program-starter? Are you known to be—even occasionally—gracious, moody, overly competitive, brainy, aesthetically inclined, rude, pious, sexy, pushy, sympathetic, chickenhearted, voracious? Outside the school, what do your wisest advisers suggest for you as a vocation? How does your family size you up? There are many ways by which you can know yourself. Use them all!

- **Know your world.** Quite aside from your own abilities and likes or dislikes, where are the vital areas of activity in today's history? What movements need "the stubborn ounces of your weight?" How do you determine what is timely and worthwhile in the fields of science, politics, law, journalism, social work, art, peace, race relations, environment, feminism, psychology, music, gay rights, or the dozens of other subjects into which a life can be invested?

Perhaps you prefer to be on the sidelines or in a quiet supporting role. On the other hand, you may want to participate directly in the main thrust of reform or development to pioneer and to stake out new areas of human concern. You can choose between reading the news rather than the comics, between hearing lectures and watching reality television. Many of us have the problem of being overloaded with local details and news stories, but knowing little about global affairs and the arena of ideas. A newsmagazine gave a summary of the main events of the past fifty years and many a reader was astonished: "Is that what was important then? I had no idea it was even taking place, even though I went through our newspaper every evening." Be as well-informed as possible about what does go on in the fast-moving history of our time.

- **Be open.** This can involve opening up your mind and imagination and your will, and in the process keeping in tune with all that happens around you. Moreover, anyone concerned with reli-

gion will naturally pray about clues and inspiration. What is God saying to you inwardly? Your willingness to accept new ideas may point you to seemingly outlandish fields of interest. Look at a wide range of lifestyles and duties. To be open keeps you aware of an unlimited variety of opportunities.

An important footnote needs to be added to every such set of vocational suggestions: nowadays many people change occupations several times during a lifetime. These changes may be unpredictable. So now we are really choosing not a life work so much as accepting our first job, with the idea of later variations. Never in history has there been such mobility in occupations. Few of us are locked in, permanently, to one kind of work. We play the field of occupational opportunity. Prepare for that mobility and expect it.

Among Protestants and Catholics, one of the oldest (and surely the corniest) stories is about the young man who said he had seen "G.P.C." written in gigantic letters in the sky and knew that they meant, "Go Preach Christ." After hearing him preach, one kindly old gentleman suggested that actually the letters might have meant, "Go Plow Corn."

How unmistakable, indeed, must a call to a career in religion be? A Bible verse reads, "Many are called but few are chosen." This follows the pattern with which we have been dealing. Various groups and denominations stipulate that even after meeting every other requirement for ordination, a person must be wanted and chosen by a congregation before the final step is taken. That is, the candidate may be sure of being called, but fails at this point in being chosen. Both factors are needed.

Yet every religious tradition agrees that anyone's claim to have divine calling to professional religious work demands full respect.

Even in history, when every outward indication seemed to show a person to be definitely not called, the person involved actually turned out to be a notable leader.

Years ago the writer of this book visited a hundred campuses, interviewing several thousand students interested in careers in religion. Frequently he was assured by a local official, "Joe believes he has a call. But we all know he'll never make it. As you are here just briefly, will you tell him that? We haven't the heart to." But not even a visiting "authority" can tell an individual that he or she hasn't received the call to religious service.

Women as Clergy

Efforts to screen out persons who claim a calling have been nowhere so controversial as in decisions about ordaining women. Until the latter half of the twentieth century, most major groups within the Jewish, Catholic, and Protestant communities never seriously considered the question. Yes, women could become members of convent orders among Catholics, though the celebrating of Mass by them, of course, was denied. In Protestant groups, even though women have traditionally comprised the majority of members and have been notably active in parish programs and financial support, ordination was not acceptable. Jewish congregations were similarly unready to ordain any women until recently. Most organized religions have through all the centuries been a purely patriarchal situation dominated by men.

Change in this tradition has been slow, but now that it has begun, it is moving faster and faster. Beginning about 1875, some Congregational and Baptist groups ordained women, and Disciples started in 1888. In the twentieth century, other groups also began to allow women to become pastors.

Although men still hold the great majority of pastoral positions, an increasing number of women now serve as ministers or rabbis. According to the U.S. Department of Labor, more than 43,000 women describe their occupation as clergy, and it is estimated that between 12 and 15 percent of clergy are female. According to the United Methodist Church News Service, more than 7,800 women serve as United Methodist ministers, holding about one out of every six pastoral positions. In the Episcopal Church there were no women priests in 1973, but by 1998 almost 14 percent of priests were women, according to figures compiled by Louie Crew of Rutgers University. In Baptist, Presbyterian, and Unitarian congregations, among others, women ministers are becoming increasingly common.

Despite a succession of large conferences and assemblies advocating the ordination of women, Roman Catholics have made no move in that direction. The papacy has continued to be cold to this idea, as well as to the idea of departing from the tradition of celibacy among priests. This is one of the points of sharpest disagreement in current Catholicism.

Jewish groups have gradually shifted ground in a liberalizing direction. Orthodox Judaism and Conservative Judaism once ordained no women. The million-member Reform Judaism movement first admitted a woman to the rabbinate in 1972, while the smaller Reconstructionist movement, and the still smaller Leo Baeck school, moved ahead with similar caution. Today, the number of women rabbis is still relatively small, but the numbers are increasing. At just one institution, Hebrew Union College, nearly four hundred women have been ordained in the last thirty years.

Such a brief overview omits reference to Christian groups such as the Orthodox (who do not ordain women) and the Pentecostals (among whom there are many well-received women clergy). But

dramatic changes in the general pattern of male supremacy in nearly all religious groups cannot be expected soon.

Pressures by Catholic parishes for the too-few ordained men are a factor in calling for the ordination of women. Many students in Catholic seminaries are women, a further factor that might relax restrictions. In the groups that do ordain women, some women find they still have an uphill fight. One of the handfuls of female Jewish clergy gave an account of the commendation she received from the president of her congregation: "I had been wonderful, he said. My services had been terrific, my sermons were outstanding, the religious schools sensational, but, he said, next year we would feel more comfortable with a man." The pattern among many Protestants is similar. Women ministers sometimes have a harder time finding a job than their male counterparts. Yet many women pastors have been so effective that it is hard to argue against ordaining more of them.

Women seeking ordination must have courage, ingenuity, and persistence. Though the ordination of women is supported by a great number of male clergy, it is women ministers, priests, and rabbis themselves who must make their way by dramatic, inspired, and compassionate filling of the clergy role in the days ahead.

Questions to Ask Yourself

Even though authorities in a congregation or national organization have their own ways of screening candidates for ordination, it is at least as urgent that men and women question themselves about their suitability for taking this step. Here are some informal, self-directed questions to ask yourself:

Do I like and get along well with people?

There is no requirement that candidates for careers in religion must be extroverted, activist, or socially out and about. But surely they cannot function successfully in their roles by being excessively shy and introverted. Tests show that men and women who are effective in such work, and who like it, are most often those who enjoy human relationships and being with people. Naturally, there is a place for scholars who may be withdrawn in attitude, and in some traditions monks and nuns have a large place. Even the solitary hermit can be helpful. But as the first paragraphs of this book emphasized, to help others is a basic motive—and liking to be with people is part of that gesture.

Do I have the potential to be a leader?

Many tasks in religion automatically place you in the forefront of your community. This is why a guidance adviser may look closely at a clergy candidate for signs of leadership abilities. Sometimes it comes about that, whereas others in the school or community are athletes, skilled musicians, or academic bright lights, someone with a low self-image decides that through religion he or she can gain instant status.

No one becomes a leader automatically. It is important that you have the competence to initiate action and to take over in an emergency, and that you are unafraid of group pressure or being labeled a nonconformist. We are often told how rare leadership is—in neighborhood politics, in club life, in school, and in the congregation. Without needing to be hero or heroine, we must ask whether we can grow into the ability to get others to act and whether we can learn to administer an active program.

Do my thoughts and my life of study enable me to interpret religious truth effectively?

To be sure, a person with great intellect but little sympathy is not preferable to a person with compassion but little intellect. However, for many centuries clergy have been the scholars, thinkers, and appraisers of the culture. Today, the field of religion calls for better-than-average brains and knowledge. It is worth noting, though, that the solid, earnest student who has worked hard to get through school usually turns out to be more useful in his or her work than the whiz kid who tosses off facts but is unimpressed with their human and spiritual meaning.

Am I physically and emotionally ready for these occupational demands?

A young woman who had built her hopes on serving in a tropical mission and had studied that country and its language was devastated to find that her health could never permit her living there. A gifted young clergyman who took spiritual depth and fire to an inner-city chapel lasted only four years before having a breakdown. A woman who had refused psychiatric treatment in college served a parish in the suburbs, only to develop phobias that unfavorably affected her performance.

Sadly, such problems are common. But the other extreme is physically and emotionally healthy people who are unable to sympathize deeply, to feel others' situations of pain or joy seriously. These individuals are also at a disadvantage for careers in religion. It is important to be equipped to feel deeply and identify with others; it is also important to be stable, vigorous, and complete as a person.

Anyone these days who has difficulty addressing issues related to sexual behavior may also face difficulties in carrying out certain duties. For example, marriage counseling is a specialization within itself. Many psychologists serve as marriage counselors. Often, couples seeking a divorce are advised by their attorneys to seek marriage counseling and to consider reconciliation. Many troubled couples prefer to confer with their pastor instead of going to a psychologist. Pastors and other religious workers should be sensitive to the causes and conflicts that threaten a marriage.

In addition, one's own beliefs and sexual orientation must be considered. Clergy and other religious professions are often under a microscope, and what some may consider one's private business may not be so private after all. Anyone planning on a religious services career must carefully consider this angle and be prepared to deal with it appropriately.

Every aspect of our lives—physical, mental, sexual, social, and spiritual—is relevant as we question our fitness. Clergy are regarded, rightly or wrongly, as providing an example of the wholeness of mind, body, and spirit. If indeed "having an ulcer means lacking deep faith in God" (a claim made by some nonulcerated people!), then all our health, inward and outward, takes on special significance.

Is my own life with religion serious and growing?

In every major religious group there is a debate about when a person is entitled to say, "This is my own belief, I now claim a relationship with God for myself." Among Jewish youth, when is a bar mitzvah too early or too late? Should Catholics allow children to come to Mass before confirmation—and when is confirmation best? For Protestants, is age twelve an appropriate time for confirmation?

Those who wonder when to declare, inwardly or outwardly, the desire for an occupation in religion, often ask the same sort of question. We would do well to be aware of the generalization that the earlier you decide, the less effective your ministry is likely to be, a conclusion reached by a team that studied the question with care. Yet even that group granted the fact that some child evangelist types become great, and that history shows us many early commitments to religion throughout the centuries.

We have also remarked that to announce one's plan for a career in religion almost invariably brings special treatment from others. In a circle of first-year college students relating what each planned occupationally, one said, "I intend to be a priest." Everyone reacted with hushed silence. But another said, "I want a job helping people, maybe as a child psychologist, teacher, social worker, priest, missionary, or recreation leader," and the response was entirely different. The second student had revealed possible motives and concerns, rather than a professional choice, and was considered as "normal" rather than "holy."

Another campus example points in the same direction. The fifteen members of a pre-theological circle were such prudish, unreal stereotypes of piety that they kept away many genuine inquirers. Yet investigation ten years later disclosed the fact that not one of these "holier-than-thou" figures actually went into a career in religion! Early commitment is not necessarily a good thing.

Another advantage of delaying outright announcement of such an occupational decision is that in many instances one's intention does change as time goes by. A young man who had decided to become a rabbi was given scholarship aid to that end, went to seminary, and there realized that this was not the life work for him at all. It seemed too late to refund the scholarship money, disappoint his family, and choose some other job field. So he went ahead into the rabbinate, unhappy and listless about his duties, until several years later he resigned. Often it is wise to leave what is sometimes known as "the hidden call" undisclosed until one is reasonably certain that it is sincere and undeniable.

What we have been saying here is that to look inward and thoroughly assess your true vocational calling makes considerable demands. It involves for most of us a great deal of reading and thinking, and a lot of self-questioning. It calls for all the aptitude and interest and psychological testing interpreted by trained counselors. It sends us off to retreats and conferences, courses and conversations, with insightful elders. These are all aspects of the process of knowing yourself, knowing the world of your chosen work, and being open to the widest and deepest prompting, divine and societal. The next logical step is to look directly at actual religious jobs and the responsibilities they entail. To this we now turn our attention.

3

CONGREGATIONAL LEADER

THIS CHAPTER WILL not continually refer to pastor, priest, and rabbi separately because in some respects these all belong together under one title. Since the middle of the twentieth century in America, the responsibilities attributed to each have flowed together and merged in an unexpected way, so that to describe one is to describe them all. Educational patterns are similar; congregational schedules, problems, and possibilities are very much alike; and the personal situations of the men or women working in these fields tend to be almost identical.

Religious groups once devoted a large part of their energies to competing with rival movements and faiths: "Our product is better!" Today such confrontations do continue, especially on television and radio, but to a notably lessened degree. We also witness a good deal of critical attention paid to the followers of the faiths that flourish alongside the more mainstream religions. Despite the nationally broadcast difficulties of television evangelists in the recent past, many of them gather great numbers of adherents.

Clergy, of course, refers to the category of employed leaders of a worshipping membership. Originally it came from the word *cleros*, meaning a portion or tithe and referring to support of the ministry by a levy or tax that everybody paid. The concept originated in Old Testament days, when laypeople brought to the temple offerings that were either to be destroyed as a sacrifice or to be eaten or sold by the clergy. This is still an aspect of the clergyperson's pay, as contract language is often worded such that he or she is "set free from worldly cares and occupations" with time to serve the group. This particular aspect of the clergy idea, which all denominations do not share nowadays, is that these persons are set aside for religious work, just as government employees are at times lifted out of the typical job world to serve their fellow citizens. In countries where there is an established church, clergy are often state-paid officials just like postmasters or police. Even though American places of worship frequently have the national flag alongside the altar or pulpit, there is actual separation of church and state. In certain European countries, however, where the congregation would not dream of having the nation's flag in the sanctuary, ministers are still paid from tax money!

Are Clergy Necessary?

Some traditions reject the idea of the clergy or priesthood; in other words, the whole notion of a set-apart ministerial profession. Quakers (the Religious Society of Friends) have refused it in most of their congregations since the seventeenth century. They point out that the title "Reverend" means "deserving of reverence," which they see as an elevation of one believer above others. Their goal, instead, has been the abolition of the laity, which means that everyone

becomes a minister. This is a respectable ideal and has led Quakers from the beginning to give women equality not only in testifying during the meetings for worship, but in filling any office or function in the group. Today many congregations of Friends do have pastors, and others pay clerks or secretaries modest salaries to serve in some sense as clergy.

Likewise, Christian Science congregations have no place for clergy. Readers and practitioners, often well remunerated for their work, serve as leaders; also there is a notable encouragement for women to take leadership, following the inspired example of Mary Baker Eddy, the American founder of the Church of Christ, Scientist, in 1879. A third nonclerical group is the Mormons (Church of Jesus Christ of Latter-Day Saints, founded in 1830 by Joseph Smith), whose growing membership of several million is led by ward officials and other full-time administrators who arrange business dealings that provide an income for the denomination.

Somewhat different is the Salvation Army—with its famous brass bands—which was begun in England in 1865 by General William Booth. Its clergy is ordained to military rank, with husband and wife equal in status at each level of command. This hardworking ministry is directed to the down-and-out and now also to a great many middle-class members. Assignments to one citadel, or meeting place, are generally six years in duration.

Among these nonclerical groups, the two founded in America—the Mormons and the Christian Scientists—are quite definite in their rejection of ordained clergy such as other groups have traditionally had. Possibly some characteristic American criticism of leaders with favored status in a local congregation played a part in that decision. Despite the fact that both faiths actually do have a well-defined group of leaders, their anticlerical origins keep some vestige of equality among members intact.

Yet these and other examples of nonclerical group organizations seem to support, rather than deny, claims that religious membership needs some full-time directorship if it is to endure. The complex, helter-skelter tempo of today's world apparently makes it imperative that some persons be employed to keep the whole religious organization and witness running.

This doesn't mean that most people want to employ somebody to act as a go-between with God, though members of the clergy are often mistakenly regarded as doing just that. Rather, it means setting one or several persons to work as gatherers of the people, as teachers, as initiators of worship, and as counselors. The clergyperson seems to have been and continues to be an integral part of civilized life, from the beginnings of civilization to the highly specialized professional situation of our modern times.

Clergy as Symbols

Another element of the clergy's importance is the need in most communities for a person to symbolize the character of the local citizenry. In the past, the word *parson* was actually a cockneylike pronunciation of the word *person*: "Who is the person in your village?" In a mysterious but understandable way, the clergyperson was and is the symbol of the town's moral values. Today, other community leaders may be excused for their dishonesty, sexual irregularity, or drunkenness, but everybody is horrified when such charges are brought against the clergy. "If they're not going to behave morally, what with all the preaching and prayer, then how can I be expected to?" Often, the virtue of the whole neighborhood seems painfully at stake.

Some members of the clergy are less than enthusiastic about this symbolic role in the neighborhood. Sometimes, discomfort at being

expected to be perfect prompts a latent rebelliousness among some clergypeople, who are tempted to live it up while on vacation or a trip, escaping from the scenario written for their behavior back home. But many members of the clergy, although not happy about being a symbol, are so relaxed and confident in their work and belief that no such overcompensation is needed. Nonetheless, anyone considering a career in religion must think about just how much an ideal, a symbol of community good behavior, he or she is willing to be. Anyone who states, "Yes, I am perfect, now that you mention it," is hardly being realistic. But anyone who says, "I resent being made a model, and either somewhere else or undercover here I'll behave with such devilishness and impurity that it would shock all the 'good people' in my town," is courting occupational disaster as well.

This same public-image decision arises in relation to clerical appearance and clothing. One determined young man said, "I want to be a clergyman, a good clergyman—but I don't want ever to look like one!" What he meant is clear to most of us as we think of the cartoon rendering of a priest, rabbi, or minister, or a sanctimonious type on the street. There is a traditional jibe at some male clergy that goes: "They want to be called 'father' but they insist on dressing like mother!" Thus, many candidates rebel at the idea of the clerical, or Roman, collar and call it (from a line in a Cardinal Newman hymn), "the encircling gloom." Some seminarians have objected that the physician doesn't wear a stethoscope on the street, nor does the chef wear a tall white hat in public, so why must clergypeople proclaim their occupation by the clothes they wear?

Others have no such hang-ups about clerical dress—just as some nuns refuse to abandon their sisterly habits in an era when many of their colleagues are adopting stylish or informal clothing. When someone needs a religious counselor or has an emergency and needs

a clergyperson, why not make it evident who such helpers are? The days when passengers on a bus or subway train rose to give their seats to a member of the clergy are apparently gone for good, and so, too, as has been mentioned, is the idea that clergypeople are reverend, a Latin word meaning "to be revered." Some are willing, even eager to be a recognizable presence amid the crowd and to indicate that organized religion is there, willing to be of service. Indeed, where the religious leader is in danger, it is a direct act of bravery and witness to appear in clerical attire.

Let us be sure that despite prejudice and many jokes, looking like a clergyperson is here to stay. A ministerial candidate in Scotland mourned that "I do hate to get ordained. I know I'll look, in a clerical collar, just like a rat peering out of a drainpipe!" But he was ready to don one all the same. It is paradoxical that at the very time when more Protestant—and some Jewish—clergy are wearing clerical dress, more Catholic priests are laying it aside to appear on the street in plain clothes. Those who do wear distinctive religious clothing often do so only when they are officiating as clergy, appearing at other times in more informal and anonymous clothing.

Each candidate for ordination these days must consult his or her own preference in such matters, taking into account traditional customs or requirements. Sometimes the person who glories in special attire is thereby demonstrating some degree of insecurity or professional inadequacy. But those who find themselves concealing the fact of their being ordained, or dressing flamboyantly to reject what in *Hamlet* are called "customary suits of solemn black," are also being less than candid.

A story in the *New Yorker* years ago told of a clergyman who was dressed in a swimsuit and relaxing by the pool at a motel. He was talking informally with another stranger and not mentioning reli-

gion in any way. When the stranger left, he said cheerily, "Well, so long, Reverend." The clergyman was struck that, lacking any visible token that he was a clergyman, he was thus spotted by his manner and attitude. Reflecting on such an incident, we may comment that if it was saintliness and an air of purity that made him recognizable, good; if it was a professional piousness that broke his disguise, it was regrettable both for the man and for the religion he served.

We should be aware that the outward trimmings, attire, and manner of the clergyperson are not the marks of his or her sincerity or authenticity. But they do change the way others regard or respond to the ministry offered. Some years ago a priest in New York serving as a Legal Aid Society lawyer was forbidden to wear clerical garb in court. The ruling was that this would be "a continuing visible communication to the jury and others in the courtroom," creating prejudice and preventing a fair trial. Yet in another case, a Chicago judge ruled that two Orthodox Jews should not have been required to remove their yarmulkes in court, because the small skullcaps are a required part of any Orthodox Jew's ordinary dress, not a proclamation of a special status. Special clothing does make a proclamation and witness, and will continue to be one of the aspects of the profession that should be thought through carefully by those considering ordination.

The Importance of Preaching

A large question for candidates for careers in religion is the place that preaching has in such jobs. Is a commanding presence or oratorical flair in the pulpit (or rostrum) a central requirement? This is an area of particular concern for men or women who find themselves with no special ability for public speaking or lacking a thundering voice.

In some religious traditions, delivering a sermon or homily has minor importance as compared with the liturgy. Members of the clergy do not exert themselves here so much with the spoken word as with the whole act of worship. In the accountings by Protestant clergy of the comparative importance of their various duties, preaching is seldom at the top of the list, even though many Protestant groups still call the minister "the preacher." In many theological schools, homiletics (the art of preaching) yields priority to the study of the religious texts, counseling, religious history, the psychology of religion, and so on.

To some extent, the demand now is for conversational preaching—informal, easy-to-understand presentations—instead of the old golden-tongued deliverance of the message once expected from the pulpit. Many preachers come down out of the pulpit to give their sermon informally at a table, or halfway down the center aisle, to avoid the appearance of talking down to the congregation. One pastor told his listeners that if they wanted great rolling sermons, they could tune these in on television or radio, whereas his goal was quiet, person-to-person teaching.

Despite criticisms of the importance and effectiveness of preaching, it continues to be a major part of the clergyperson's task. Catholics coming from Mass speak often of "Father So-and-So's wonderful homily" rather than about the music, the impressiveness of the Sacrament, or other elements of the service. The requirement since Vatican II, the Roman Ecumenical Council in the 1960s, that every celebration of Communion must be accompanied with a homily perhaps upgraded preaching more than any other Catholic action had for several hundred years.

Preaching by rabbis is known widely in America as being particularly forceful, oratorically expert, and moving to listeners of all faiths. Jewish theological school training in preaching is thorough and impressive. In many cities a rabbi exchanges pulpits once a year with a Unitarian Universalist minister, and the general reaction is that the sermons are not only similar, but matching in fire and interest. Compared to such Reform Judaism, preaching by Conservative or Orthodox rabbis, though overshadowed by chanting and ritual, is now increasingly scholarly and open to the world.

Many ministers once looked upon Protestant preaching as a fading phenomenon of the past. Other parish skills were often touted as far more relevant. Yet the advent of a great many mass-media evangelists, on the airwaves as well as in stadiums packed with listeners, unexpectedly reversed this judgment. As search committees from Protestant congregations appraise candidates, the ability to preach effectively is again paramount in most situations. Put rather crassly, in congregations where ministers are not just appointed by authority, the price tag is on preaching, as effective sermonizers move to larger and larger congregations. In downtown parishes in dozens of cities, a church may be known as a preaching post rather than the family-type suburban church where weekday social life among the group is more important. People will go a long way to hear their religion explored with color and conviction, and the preacher competes rather amazingly with the television in the comfortable living room for the loyalty of many thousands each week.

What does this durable priority of preaching say to a possible candidate whose gifts in such group communication are modest or even insufficient? Homiletics training in theological school can take unpromising preachers and bring out unsuspected powers. In many seminaries, the earnest student orating to an empty chapel or classroom after midnight is a part of this transformation. Or the quiet-voiced speaker who learns to master the microphone sometimes gains force and clarity for nonamplified speaking as well. More importantly, the student who urgently has something to say will be heard and will be effective. The sermon outline, alertness to people's questions and problems, eye contact with person-to-person intensity—these are part of growth in preaching that is available to anyone dedicated to the task.

The idea is to neither downgrade preaching nor make it the whole of a clergyperson's work, but to keep its importance in perspective. Suffice it to say that despite all its variations and departures (the careless sermon, the drive-in outdoor sermon, the radio sermon, the droning manuscript sermon, the no-eye-contact sermon, the all-quotes sermon, the tired sermon), preaching is undoubtedly here to stay. It is a skill to be cultivated by anyone seeking to serve an effective role in religion.

Thus far we have discussed the necessity for clergy, the symbolic values it serves among people today, and the special aspect that preaching gives to the clergyperson's skills portfolio. Now let's look at a cross section of what the leader of a congregation actually does in modern-day churches and temples.

The Urban Congregation

Among Roman Catholic churches, the great bulwark in America is the downtown parish. Here a typical staff may be made up of seven members. Four might be men, and three women—three priests, two sisters, one single person (more likely a woman and possibly an ex-nun), and one married person, who may be a permanent deacon or a lay member of a parish council or committee. Characteristically, these persons serve in a massive and often venerable church, with a parochial school next door. In the suburbs, because there's more space and the communities are generally newer, the large place of worship is more modern, often of striking architectural design, and has a centered table, unobtrusive confession booths, cameolike stations of the cross, a crying room for infants, and a baroque organ with exposed pipes.

Protestant congregations of the same general community have similar staffs: several ordained clergy plus others with responsibility for education, music, maintenance, and secretarial duties. One large denomination specifies that there should be one clergyperson for every 750 members; when the congregation reaches that size, another is to be added. Downtown offices are customarily open all day, even if the main worship building is closed on weekdays. The sanctuary is flanked by corridors that contain church schoolrooms, a lounge or two, kitchens, and sometimes a gymnasium or bowling lanes. The minister's study often adjoins the library.

Jewish places of worship in metropolitan areas have become increasingly similar in facilities and in numbers of staff personnel. There are generally several rabbis, secretaries, cantors, organists, and maintenance employees. Here, as in the other faiths, there is an administrative angle to the work of the responsible rabbi.

Any large congregation of any faith must make provision for a steady volume of telephone calls and off-the-street visitors or persons in need. Members expect home visits, especially at times of crisis. Teaching children, supervising a day nursery, persuading those with less experience to lead classes or share committee chores, coordinating financial campaigns, keeping the calendar of endless weekday and Sunday meetings, preparing bulletins and often a congregational newsletter, and maintaining the buildings are all respon-sibilities that must be assigned to various members of the staff.

Most members of the congregation, however, see their clergy just once a week, and even then only up front. So they often wonder what such a worker does between worship times, how she or he ful-fills duties on weekdays? To give you some indication of the busy schedule of a leader of a congregation, let's look at an ordinary day in his or her life.

A Typical Day in a Religious Leader's Life

The alarm clock goes off at 7:00 A.M., because by 8:00 A.M., the religious leader must be downtown to lead a businesspeople's reli-gion class at breakfast—twenty men and women who have met weekly for years at a coffee shop. By 9:15, when he or she gets back to the study, the secretary has already received several phone calls. One is to ask the leader to come at once to the General Hospital, where a young man is in bad shape after a car crash the night before. Another is from a newspaper asking for a comment for or against the new civic housing program. A third is from the manager of the congregation's camp in the mountains, asking whether a seventy-two-inch freezer will be big enough for that facility. A fourth call is a request for a single sentence in a proposed leaflet about nuclear disarmament.

Before these phone calls are attended to, any E-mail messages must also be read and answered. Then the mail, opened and placed on the desk, demands attention, too:

"Dear Leader: Our Rotary Club, just twenty miles from the city, wants a hard-hitting talk on the spiritual basis of democracy. Would your schedule permit . . ."

"Dear Leader: My father-in-law heard your sermon last week and asked me to get from you the Socrates quote you used near the end."

"Dear Leader: Because your assistance in the college fund drive was what really put us over the top, the trustees have voted that out of gratitude for your service to the cause of higher education, we wish to confer on you an honorary degree at our next commencement."

"Dear Leader: Why don't you preach real religion and leave social issues alone? You clergy have no business meddling in matters of politics, race, nuclear armament, global warming, or other subjects that the chamber of commerce or the legislature is better equipped to handle! Stay busy with that flock of yours. Don't waste your ministry and your congregation's money interfering with the world."

"Dear Leader: Your congregation's gift of $20,000 to our charity program was so helpful that the board would like to ask whether next year your generous grant might even be increased."

"Dear Leader: One of the five young men for whom you have been serving as parole sponsor has now completed his three-year probation period, and I am sending him to you about job possibilities."

"Dear Leader: Why struggle along with an old-fashioned, wheezy pipe organ, when for a few thousand dollars your place of worship can have a brand-new electronic instrument, with simulated chime attachment? Read the enclosed circular . . ."

"Dear Leader: What you did and said last month when my dear wife died helped pull me through. How can I begin to express . . ."

"Dear Leader: This is to report that the psychiatric counselor to whom you sent me has given me therapy that has helped me deal successfully with my neurosis. Until you spotted what was wrong, nobody had a clue, and I am grateful . . ."

"Dear Leader: Our forum program again wants to have a panel (rabbi, priest, and pastor) speak about the latest Middle East developments. You have been suggested as one who could . . ."

Such a stack of letters or E-mails could be multiplied indefinitely and is an indication of how the leader of a city or suburban congregation "finds" something to do between weekly services. There may be no time during the day for the dictating machine, so replies often have to be dictated late at night. Morning time must often be given to study and to preparing the week's sermon as well as other talks and addresses, and the rest of the world must sometimes be shut out to get such necessary work done. And before having lunch at home nearby, there is that quick visit to the hospital.

Afternoon finds our subject stopping at one of the service clubs to advocate for the proposed charity drive. Next come visits to a half-dozen homes or offices—many of the calls ending with a short sentence of prayer, which is expected. Supper is provided at a downtown hotel by the city's Council of Churches, with nearly all the Protestant, Catholic, and Jewish groups represented. After that there is a stop at an area youth rally, where the clergyperson has been requested to give a five-minute inspirational talk about teenage drinking.

After such a day, returning to the rectory/parsonage/manse, or residence, is not yet to be. A few minutes at a fiftieth-wedding-anniversary reception is a must, with a word of blessing to help make it memorable. At day's end, the 11:00 P.M. news, usually summarizing the world's woes, is a fitting prelude to prayers at bedtime.

"Is it like this every day?" a church member asked wonderingly after checking in on such a schedule for a single twenty-four-hour period.

"Days just aren't long enough," shrugs our subject. "And every chore seems important. Even if I weren't paid a cent for any of it, I'd want to do it. Is this city any better because of all this involvement of mine? I can't say. But I am doing my best to see that maybe I bring some comfort to someone each day."

The Small-Town Congregation

Just as the tempo of life outside major population centers is slower, clergy work here is usually less hectic than downtown or in a suburb. But because a congregational leader is personally better known and more visibly available in a village, the timetable can be a busy one—especially in a rural setting, where everybody might know the clergyperson, and there is no place for him or her to be anonymous.

In less-populated places, the leader of a congregation is often called to serve more than one charge. Sometimes this is because there is a shortage of clergy, as has been the case among Catholics in many regions. More often, it is because a small group of members, unless they have a grant from some mission headquarters, can't support a full-time leader. Among Protestants, there is an advantage here for so-called connectional denominations, in which a bishop or other executive can combine congregations, assign personnel, and often pay the bill, whereas a largely congregational form of government allows each group to go its own way and frequently to dissolve entirely. The two-point, three-point, or grueling many-point arrangement for one clergyperson can be called "linked," "yoked," "a larger parish," or (for an interdenominational pattern) "a federated parish."

As might be expected, these rural situations in American religious life are usually served by clergy who either are new to the field, so that they can gain experience in a less demanding role, or are nearing retirement and thus are attracted to the slower pace. Men or women just out of seminary, with abundant energy, may be found here, too. Retired clergy, with wisdom and skill but lessened vitality, may serve part-time or in a relaxed schedule. Thus it is in the small congregations that leaders from both ends of the age spectrum do much of the work—a situation paralleled in small congregations in the inner city, where budgets are minimal.

It is true, however, that today a seemingly growing number of clergy members steadily prefer and rejoice in the rural, small-town, or middle-sized-town ministry. The salary is modest, even with members' gifts of corn, tomatoes, and preserves added in. But these clergypeople believe that the more intimate group, the open community, the less-polluted environment, the smaller schools, and the lighter professional load are all rewarding. Clergy members have in many cases refused jobs in higher-up echelons to continue their direct ministry in the smaller setting.

An interesting characteristic of the small place of worship is that there the graduated seminarian probably will make her or his most obvious mistakes in ministry. These may include such gaffes as alienating a pillar of the congregation, committing mishaps in worship, unintentionally shocking local gossips, or even preaching on wrong or naive sermon themes and teachings. From some of these errors, the leader's ministry may never be able to recover in that particular place, and he or she must simply go elsewhere and start again. Thus, after two or three years, partly at the prompting of superiors in the area organization, it is usual for the clergyperson, possibly sadder but wiser, to leave. Of course, this is not always the situation; many find their first assignment the most exciting of their lives.

Progress toward larger goals for the priest, minister, or rabbi usually starts here. The determining factors include ambition, professional preference, the decisions of superiors, and demonstrated effectiveness, such as good preaching, skilled counseling, or masterful administration. After that first location for two or so years, the second assignment is often for five years (this is a fast-growth point, where vigor is in demand), the third for ten years (where there is solid building of the ministry), then possibly a fourth place for fifteen years, with more relaxed duties thereafter until retirement. This succession of moves customarily begins in a rural or small-town congregation, though first involvement may also be an assistantship position with a large-city church or temple.

There are no absolutes about the comings and goings of clergy members in their jobs. Some may choose to stay in their first charge for decades; others choose to make frequent changes. Yet others may suspend their ordained service for various periods of nonordained, secular work. Many are "under orders" for the duration of their ministry, that is, they are occupationally secure but lacking freedom to move as they choose. Those under no authority but their own (and that of a single congregation) obviously have far less security but boundless liberty in the whole field.

Some leaders of congregations in small or middle-sized communities find a special virtue in staying and working there. The small congregation, they say, is the one primary group left in a fast-shifting American culture. Sociologists tell us that the genuine community has crumbled or been swept away by a whole series of factors: the consolidated school instead of the community "little red schoolhouse," the supermarket instead of the local general store, swift job mobility instead of settled work in one place, fast travel on good roads instead of relative isolation, and easily obtained divorce instead of a couple's old-fashioned determination to work things out. Amid all this, in thousands of areas, the church, mosque, or temple is the one remaining center for real community: the neighbor-to-neighbor, hand-to-hand, eye-to-eye, week-to-week concern of one human being for another. As the English writer G. K. Chesterton used to remind us, "To make it live, make it local!"

Nothing takes the place of the congregational supper, at which many families bring their own contribution to the total menu. Nothing replaces the weekly hour or so when there are moments of complete silence in a worshipping group, children among parents whose heads are bowed in reverence, group singing, and sometimes dancing with others whom we all recognize. Nothing sounds like the bell calling rich and poor, wise and simple, young and old, to gather and acknowledge the deepest truths in themselves and in the universe. To foster and deepen this experience of community, with all its renewing of the best in people, is a remarkably significant service to the future of the nation and the human race.

Who else but the pastor relates people to people in this way in today's world? Physicians often counsel and uphold others. Teachers gather children and youth and shape their growth. The county agricultural agent, organizing the area Future Farmers or 4-H Club, can be important. Recreation directors, coaches, and sometimes police are in many cases effective in community building. But the one place where every sector of the populace is welcome to take part is the church, mosque, or temple. Without judging anyone's theology or sacramental adequacy, we are well aware that achieving people-with-people togetherness is vital to political democracy and the human future.

Some readers may object here that these points have little to do with the direct witness of religious truth. Are we merely called to gather and deepen some sort of social togetherness in North American society? By no means! Rather, this is all part of the religious task of wholeness and health, both mental and spiritual. Even the tiny congregation in any neighborhood is a nucleus, a gathering point, a haven, a demonstration of the good that religious service can achieve.

The Need for More Religion Professionals

In choosing an occupation, the normal course is to make sure that there are openings in the field that concerns you. Are there enough certified public accountants? Mechanical engineers? Web designers? Often young people get the impression that the ranks of nearly all workers are already filled up, with little or no room for replacements. Do we face a surplus of persons in religious service, too? Even for the person who finds a definite call in his or her life, this is a particularly relevant question.

Dangers do exist in relying on statistics. If you choose a career in a church or temple solely because you hear there are a lot of empty pulpits, you are on dubious ground. On the other hand, there is good sense in finding what the supply and demand picture is among the ranks of clergypeople.

No simple statistics are available. To give figures relevant for the years in which this book may be useful is more difficult than ever before. Ever since World War II, personnel needs in religion have been chaotic and fast-changing. So each candidate must refer to her or his own national organization for definite projections. For instance, this is particularly true with the Orthodox Christian groups: Russian Orthodox, Greek Orthodox, Serbian Eastern Orthodox, Eastern Orthodox Catholic, Holy Ukrainian Orthodox, Romanian Orthodox Episcopate, Syrian Orthodox, Turkish Orthodox, and others. Many such ethnic congregations (as the younger generation in America has grown up with little or no knowledge of the old language or tradition) are in need of new leadership. If you were associated with one of these groups, it would be worthwhile to start by asking members of your clergy for information about the situation.

Despite all such unknowns about numbers, some sort of overall summary may be suggested:

1. Some Protestant groups have a surplus of clergy. In others, demand is growing as fewer people enter seminaries. In some denominations, the number of young people entering the ministry has declined, to be replaced in part by older adults who have taken on ministry as a midlife career change.
2. In the Roman Catholic Church, there has been a constant shortage. In some sectors this shortage is serious.
3. Jewish groups—Orthodox, Conservative, Reform, and Reconstructionist—find demand fairly equal with supply.

Roman Catholic Supply and Demand

As any concerned American knows, there has been extensive Catholic readjustment since the Vatican II council of the 1960s, which sought to "update" (*aggiomamento* is the Italian and Vatican term) or modify the wording, and to some degree the meaning, of the liturgy. This temporarily confused millions of worshipers but satisfied leaders and observers who wanted to see the Church open up to the modern world. Mass is now a joyous meal eaten by believers around a table, rather than sacred elements handed down from an altar. Hymns are sung by the congregation, not just by choirs or cantors. Not Latin but the local language (the "vernacular") is the language of worship. Married deacons are admitted to the chancel sanctuary. Women take part in various holy functions there. Fasting on Friday and the age-old custom of fasting during Lent are no longer required.

At that same time, other factors were coming into play. Many minor seminaries for candidates for the priesthood and the orders started closing down, as the educational pattern became first college, then seminary. There was a notable breaking down of the barriers separating clergy and laity, for example, priests and nuns exchanging their clerical garb for street attire. And in recent years, serious problems such as abuse of children by a few priests have also been a negative factor. Some fear that the negative publicity will deter even more young people from choosing a religious career.

One unforeseen result of these inspired but bewildering changes has been a steady decline in the number of applicants for the priesthood and for the men's and women's orders. Thousands of clergypeople and men and women in orders simply withdrew from their ordained life. This perplexing movement apparently peaked around 1970, as a great exodus took place and many former clergy even married. Monasteries and convents that previously had turned down inquirers were falling widely short of their minimum expectations. Hundreds of parochial schools closed down, partly because of the cost of employing the secular teachers needed to replace the unpaid monks and nuns who had resigned.

Meanwhile, as in all religious groups, there was an upsurge of anti-Church thinking. Movies and television overwhelmingly endorsed secular lifestyles. Family ties became loosened, despite conferences and campaigns to restore the Catholic family. Even the traditional pride of parents having a son or daughter ordained has been widely eroded. One might say that never in its history has the Roman Catholic Church undergone such a time of questioning and such an exodus of clergy and teachers.

According to the U.S. Department of Labor, there are about forty-five thousand priests in the United States today. This compares to approximately fifty-eight thousand in 1965, according to statistics compiled by *U.S. News and World Report*. During the same period, the number of Catholics has grown from about forty-five million to more than sixty million. Meanwhile, enrollment in Catholic theological schools has fallen. An article in the *Naples Daily News* reported that enrollment in American seminaries has dropped from more than eight thousand in 1968 to about thirty-five hundred today.

Linking such declines with the prophetic adjustments of the tradition enacted at Vatican II is a complicated conjecture. Has worship itself been disrupted for young people? Have the replacement of many parochial schools by catechism centers and secular influence in Catholic colleges made a difference in vocations? Has the general secularization of contemporary life been responsible? Has the traditional appeal of orders, clergy status, the collar, or the professional priesthood been somehow lost? In a culture so dedicated to sexual expression as ours is, has celibacy pushed a lot of people away from the priesthood?

Can it be that, instead of being attracted to the profession by the status of the ordained clerical life, young people in future days will be impelled toward the Church (Catholic and otherwise) by the need to help secular forces in democracy deal with the crucial problems of our day? These problems, many thoughtful young people declare, include world peace and disarmament, energy, race conflict, chronic unemployment, conservation of the earth, alienation caused by an impersonal society, and the inane quality of higher education that lacks values. Seminary teachers claim that their best students cling far less today to meticulously administered holy rites and find their new vision through activist movements.

Protestant Supply and Demand

As has been suggested, patterns in this sector of the religious map are less definite and available than are those for Catholics. In Chapter 2, we looked at figures about women in various denominations and noted the fast-rising number of ordained women in each. But such statistics do not help us much in deciding how many more clergy might be needed in the future.

Several developments, however, do have a direct bearing on the number of career opportunities available. With many budgets reduced and inflation a constant deterrent, many parishes that used to have several ministers on their staff have had to make do with fewer. So assistantships, which provided first assignments every year for hundreds of graduating seminarians, are far less available. At the same time, seminaries of almost all groups have been training a large number of women, who as we have seen are gradually being welcomed as pastors. Another circumstance has been the merging of many churches: those that formerly had two or three pastors among them now have only one.

Some Protestant groups do have a shortage of pastors. Parishes still segregated for Hispanics and African-Americans—a situation many hope is changing fast—need leaders with special language and cultural understanding. But a large proportion of such churches prefers not just seminary-graduated ministers, but ministers with zeal and drama.

Many of the fastest-growing so-called Protestant congregations are part of the strongly evangelical, Pentecostal, "Bible believing" movement. There, ordained leaders usually need not have college or seminary in their training; only a year or two of Bible institute study suffices.

Conceivably, the large Protestant groups may become reinvigorated in the future. The founding of new churches and the renewal of old ones, special programs for new population challenges, missionaries sent and paid for by growing congregations—these may yet be on the drawing board. Such changes could well use all the candidates who offer themselves.

The surer means by which the pastoral positions will become available is by the loss due to retirement and death of a large number of clergy. Thousands must be replaced yearly. But in the fast-moving religious and employment currents of the days ahead, no one can foretell whether there may be large losses among the clergy or large growth of membership. Some observers sound the warning: Protestant clergy in the near future may be in far shorter supply, numerically, than Catholic priests and monastics are now.

Part-Time Ministries

Part-time ministries, customary in some communities now, may become even more common in the future. The phrase "tent-making ministry" derives from the Apostle Paul, the notable missionary of the early church who continued to earn money by his original occupation of tent making, even while he was heavily engaged in ministry. The pattern translates to our time when a man or woman cannot be fully paid by a church group, but nonetheless wants to serve among those in the group while holding a paying secular job.

For some persons this type of ministry is a reassertion of the Quaker belief mentioned earlier: all members of the congregation are ministers, with the ordained one not set apart from others. It becomes a way of affirming the common identity of Christians, all being called to an everyday job, and all called as well to duties in the congregation. As we have seen, this equalization has strong American roots, because ordination has often seemed to set one person spiritually above others.

As an example of how such part-time ministry can be fruitful, consider the case where two professionals apply for a single job. They ask that each of them be paid a half salary for half-time work, with the rest of their time devoted to family activities and social and political concerns. Simplicity of living standards enables both heads of households to get along satisfactorily with the half salary.

Will such tent making become more widely accepted among ordained leaders? It may. Men or women who quit business and enter seminary often exult: "It's great to be able to give all my time to doing what I most care about!" The full-time aspect of the ministry is essential for them. And many a layperson can be relieved to leave churchly chores to a professional who is paid to do nothing else.

The alternative of tent making combined with religious work is a thoughtful option. In history, it has allowed many devoted individuals to work several years at an ordained job without pay while supporting themselves with secular jobs. Of course, this practice is not without its drawbacks. For example, can one return full-time to the secular working world without loss of status or seniority? Is there enough energy and time for two jobs?

Supply and Demand for Rabbis

Any reader for whom ordained Jewish ministry has an appeal will come from one of the four great traditions of Jewish belief and life in this country: Orthodox, Conservative, Reform, and Reconstructionist. Facts and figures about the employment picture for each are available from their national offices.

A rabbi is often described as "a Jewish priest." This is an error, because in Judaism priesthood belongs only with the Temple in Jerusalem, where it has not yet been restored. Rather, the rabbi is a teacher, an announcer of the law, and an interpreter of the law. It has been almost exclusively a man's role, although as has been mentioned, women rabbis have been ordained in liberal branches of Judaism.

The preaching done by rabbis is similar to that done by the Christian clergy, but without the aim of converting or winning over outsiders. Rather, the intention here is to gather in the many Jews who have become largely secularized and for whom Judaism is merely an inherited ethnic and cultural brotherhood. How are such estranged Jews to be brought back under the Covenant? When a Jewish youth formally becomes a member of the congregation (the ceremony for this status is called *bar mitzvah* for boys and *bat mitzvah* for girls), fallen-away Jewish friends share the celebration and may often be reached for deeper commitment to Judaism. Intellectual and artistic events at a Jewish community center provide the rabbi and educator additional opportunities to witness.

Although Jews comprise less than 5 percent of the American population, the influence of Judaism is deep and pervasive in education, psychology, music, law, and business. Even after Hitler and the Holocaust, which helped to strengthen the spiritual roots of many Jews, a large proportion of Jews are still not "religious" Jews. Every rabbi, like his or her Christian counterparts, may take special interest in encouraging persons to active participation in the religious tradition.

By most predictions, those subscribing to the Jewish faith are gradually decreasing in number. The reasons for this decline include smaller families, intermarriage, and other ways of merging with the gentile world, and above all, the same pervasive secularism that affects every other religious group.

It is in this atmosphere that candidates for the rabbinate now hear the ancient *qahal*. The option is an urgent one for able Jews, men or women, concerned for the vitality of their faith.

The Pastor's or Rabbi's Role

After looking at these sketches of the situation of clergy in the three main traditions, let's go on to sum up the leading characteristics of members of the clergy as we see them today. Some of the comments are favorable, some unfavorable. The purpose of these discussions is not to recruit anyone for such occupations. Rather, the intent is to inform, to prompt further investigation, and to point to aspects of the whole field that may be of vocational interest.

The various functions of the clergy have long been sorted out in several rather inevitable categories. They may be called teachers, pastors, priests, or prophets. These central responsibilities are much more important than some others to which reference has already been made, such as community errand runner or symbol of virtue or even (spare the term) gatherer of the primary sociological group. Look at these roles in succession, weighing them in the light of your own experience and expectations.

Teacher

For centuries, the teacher in every community was the clergyperson. Scholarship and priesthood went together, even in pagan religions; this religious leader was the one member of the group who had ample opportunity to study the inherited scrolls, parchments, or hieroglyphics. During the first centuries of the Christian era, it was the monks, priests, and sisters in monasteries who maintained the life of learning, copied and recopied manuscripts, taught the novices, and carried on the rare tradition of reading and writing.

When the Protestant Reformation came to Europe, the clergy still did the educational work of every hamlet or town. The aim was that everyone should be taught to read and write, initially so that all could study the Bible for themselves. To achieve this, the parson became the schoolmaster. In colonial America especially, this preacher-teacher combination continued, with the early academies in New England and Middle Atlantic towns being church-affiliated.

The whole idea of universal public education began in Geneva, Switzerland, under the guidance of John Calvin, a lawyer-theologian. Indeed, it was only in later nineteenth-century America that schools became separated from churches and the clergy, and the concept of secular public education began to take shape. Until then, all schooling had been parochial.

This teaching tradition has been a definite by-product of a certain kind of religious ideal. Catholics in America, unwilling to trust public education to shape their children's ideas, kept to their parish schools even after free schooling, paid for by tax money, was made available to all citizens. Thus the teaching responsibility of Catholic clergy is, by definition, heavier than that of Protestant leaders, who are committed to the secular public schools merely aided by Sunday school. Incidentally, Sunday school itself was begun long before public education, in the early nineteenth century, to "save" children whose parents had let slide the original Protestant practice of home Bible instruction. Through all these historical developments, there arose the famous "separation of Church and State" clause, which was written into the United States Constitution to ensure that there would be no established national religion such as European nations had.

The clergyperson as teacher has thus been replaced, for the majority of the population, as the one charged with communicating facts in the secular realm, though clergy still retain the main responsibility for religious instruction. The national arguments in America about the use of prayers in public schools often mean that anything having to do with religion must be left to the church or temple and not allowed in the secular place of learning. Advocates of some sort of classroom worship, on the contrary, insist that this practice is far from advocating an established religion. Without it, they say, many students will fail to realize that religion plays an integral part in the learning experience.

Doubtless the most important vehicle for religious instruction is the weekly worship service and its Scripture, hymns, liturgy, and sermon or homily. Many churches now provide Bibles in the pews, or even the day's lessons printed on a bulletin sheet, and the instructional aim of the service is plain. A new insistence in many Protestant groups is that the sermon, which formerly was on any theme the preacher might choose, must follow directly after the reading of the Gospel, upon which the sermon is intended to be a commentary and interpretation. There is also teaching in the hymns and chants. Teaching is further set forth in stained-glass windows, as it has been for many hundreds of years. Recent innovations in many churches have included the use of large banners illustrating various texts and teachings, the use of computer projection devices, and other visual aids. The whole service of worship, to the eye of the educator, can be construed as a time of learning, reminding, and declaring.

More instruction takes place in courses taught by the clergy in the church school, in adult classes, in confirmation or communicant classes, and possibly even in the weekday nursery class. In larger congregations, a director of religious education is given much of this responsibility, but no matter what the size of the group, the clergyperson is the pivotal teacher of the parish program.

Can she or he teach skillfully and earnestly? Whether in seminary or elsewhere, has this person fully mastered the ideas and history so that he or she can convincingly present the Word? Are there enough books, periodicals, and other aids; enough translations of Scripture; and sufficient illustrations and charts and audiovisual or computer aids to enable the clergy members to do their teaching job well? As public schools present material with every kind of allurement ("Adventures with Numbers" instead of "arithmetic"), religious teaching must also be more than drab, rote memorization. The clergy must compete with the ingenious methods of instruction that children and adults get in schools and through the fascinating offerings of TV, movies, and the Internet.

Just as rabbis are teachers and not priests, by the same token other clergy should realize how vital is the teaching function they are called to uphold. As Chaucer said admiringly of the clergy in the *Canterbury Tales*, "gladly wolde he lerne, and gladly teche." Any clergyperson may well rejoice in both these elements of his or her calling.

Pastor

The Latin word for pastor is "shepherd," bringing to mind the picture of a herder with a flock gathered around. Incongruously, there often appears in a stained-glass window the nameplate *Pastor Bonus* (which means "good shepherd"), which ordinary members might unknowingly think has something to do with a larger salary for the clergyperson! Actually, the term must not be taken literally: the relationship between shepherd and real sheep is often characterized by rough treatment given to a stupid and wayward group by a superior being. Yet despite its antiquated origins, the word pastor is a term that in modern usage carries overtones of caring, wise guidance, healing, and even redemption. To be a good pastor—yes, a sheepherder—is high praise for the clergyperson.

When seeking assurance through another's concern, compassion, and sage advice, many people hold deep respect for pastors. This book mentioned at the outset the fact that most people in trouble first go to a religious counselor for help. Such pastoral care may take place in the study or office, in the home, hospital, preschool playground, retirement home, funeral parlor, prison, college lounge, airliner seat, or golf course—anywhere a pastor goes. It is a quiet, steady upholding. The good pastor is neither a compulsive conversationalist nor a silent, oracular authority. Even in a Catholic confessional, unseen, the priest conveys real interest in the problems and shortcomings of the person confessing. In fact, if he or she is not emotionally worn out after a series of problem-wrestling talks, something is lacking in his or her dedication.

Some decades ago, psychiatrists and others taught seminarians to be outwardly unmoved in dealing with troubled individuals. The point was, at all costs, to avoid being shocked or upset by whatever had been related.

Nowadays the expression of empathy is more the norm. It is taken for granted that those in need come to the clergyperson genuinely troubled, possibly for very serious reasons. The pastor cannot abandon personal convictions about what is right or wrong, good or bad; but it is essential for the pastor to accept the person who is seeking his or her counsel. The pastor must take both the person and the crisis seriously, not putting anyone down but upholding and dignifying that person.

Developing skills and confidence for such pastoral functions has been an aim of much seminary training for decades. Courses are offered in pastoral theology, in counseling, and in every aspect of the care of the parish or congregation. An extremely practical part of a seminarian's education (required in many schools) is enrollment for a summer, semester, or school year in a training program under the staff chaplain of a hospital. Members of a trainee group of a dozen or so are often scathingly frank and usually very helpful. Comments by the staff add to the impact. Reports of visits to patients, presented verbatim, are given critical attention in the group seminar, often with amazingly helpful analyses of just where the interview went off the track.

The thoroughness of such training, sometimes reinforced later by refresher courses, is indicative of the seriousness with which counseling is regarded within today's clergy. For it has often been found that when a clergyperson is naive, uninstructed, inappropriately blunt, evangelistic at an inopportune time, or hampered with some sort of personal hang-up, great harm can result for members of a congregation and others.

Even more essential than pastoral skills is the basic integrity of the clergyperson. Prayer, deference to others, complete and trusted confidentiality, unselfish concern, coveting people for God—these are the qualities and abilities required of priest, rabbi, and minister in the pastoral role.

Priest

Older than any other function of the clergy is the contribution of the priest to a congregation. In many cultures, as we have observed, the priest is the go-between who links the Deity to the tribe or nation. The priest maintains sacredness in objects and words and individuals, and makes members of the group acceptable to that Deity. Because of the key role in this process, the priestly figure is usually a part of the establishment, and he or she deals with those who have political and societal control.

Again and again, such priests have done battle with prophets. Priests, and sometimes priestesses, supported by the government or by temple offerings, have over the centuries tended to bless and sanctify whatever the rules and ruling classes have desired. They usually live well, enjoy special favors, intone the worship services by the book, and variously represent the religious aspects of officialdom. In sharp contrast—in Zion or Cuzco or Washington—the prophet, who usually comes from among the common people—as did Moses or Joan of Arc—is aware of a call to do certain things in the name of truth, justice, and the Lord. Coming to the royal court, the prophet cries disapproval of the easy life there and thunders denunciation upon hypocrisy and injustice.

Priestly types, in the rebellious youth of the developing nation of America, have often been unwelcome. Early missionary Catholic fathers were admired for heroism and self-sacrifice, rather than for the ordained powers they possessed. As previously mentioned, the two large religious movements founded in this country, Mormonism and Christian Science, have emphatically renounced the idea of priests. When for some years at the White House a succession of court preachers was announced, there was much negative comment. When Protestant or Catholic leaders make a pontifical or authoritarian claim, public reaction is usually hostile. If big-income figures for a clergyperson are made public, the common response is critical. Apparently in this country, where separation of church and state is traditional, identification of religious leaders with government power (the usual priestly linkage in established churches or Muslim countries) is frowned upon.

Ironically, Americans also insist upon various aspects of priestly cooperation with rulers. We have chaplains in the Congress opening each major session with prayer. State legislatures follow suit. As a government leader is inaugurated, a usual part of the ceremonies is also a prayer, often with invocation and benediction by clergy members of the other two religious traditions. In putting together a prestigious committee for some public cause, care is customarily taken to include someone of religious prominence. Religion has its priestly, public side in our society.

In a sense, every ministry—ordained or not—has this priestly side. It holds in reverence an objective truth and assurance that it does not originate and is not called to alter or change. In the constant conflict in Hebrew history (like that in every religion's story) between priest and prophet, it is when priests fail to respect and communicate the power of what they have been given that the prophetic voice is raised. Millions of Americans have come from lands where this outcry was heard. In fact, our chronic suspicion of the priesthood may come from prophetic claims about the believer's own personal access to our higher power.

Prophet

Are some of us called today to be prophets—possibly many of us? The young person just out of seminary often is sure about what is wrong, whereas the older religious leader is sure of what is right and admirable. One young seminarian, asked to preach to the big congregation from which he had come, delivered a fiery condemnation of many evils, demanding a radical reorienting of society and religion. Those in the congregation were aghast. Were these not statements coming from one of their own young people? He sounded so disloyal, even antireligious! Years later the former seminarian looked back and mused, "I wish I felt as strong now about anything as I did that day about everything!"

But the prophetic aspect of the ordained person's task is certainly not just a foible of naive youth. Rather, it is essential for every career in religion, if one is to arouse people and speak for God in today's world. It means making an analysis of the living situation around us from the standpoint of justice, love, and compassion, and declaring it. One member of a congregation said, "Our pastor preaches good safe sermons, but (fortunately) never anything prophetic!" We are reminded of the age-old claim that the clergy's task is "to comfort the afflicted, and afflict the comfortable," which is perhaps a prophetic definition of the job.

The place to do this, notably, is from the pulpit. Many clergy have realized, with awe and satisfaction, that the pulpit is the freest rostrum in the country. Any interpretation of truth, any warning to society, or any exhortation to change behavior can be given by the preacher who has the confidence of that particular congregation. A footnote to such preaching freedom may warn that it is free only because hearers automatically discount much of what the preacher says: "Well, we expect claims like that from clergy; I'd not respect a person in the pulpit who didn't say things like that." Or, "It's all right for him (or her) to make such demands, but the preacher doesn't need to live in my world!" Yet it is decidedly worthwhile to confront a congregation week after week with interpretations of day-to-day life. Preaching can deal with work, family, personal inner life, and news headlines around the world. It also takes in the vast resources of Scripture and many fresh aspects of divine wisdom.

Does this really apply today? Prophetic statements, especially if they are accompanied by action, disturb and annoy many people. It is part of the teaching ministry to bring people to a place in their own thinking where they will accept new mandates of the Word. A common reaction of those who resent this is to strike back at the prophetic leader. Critics ordinarily do not attack the leader's saintliness or godly claims, but find fault with something else—a mannerism, an alleged personal scandal, or a misinterpreted remark. Bishop Francis McConnell, who encouraged the clergypeople under his supervision to accept the challenge of prophetic social action, warned them: "If you act out the Gospel, take special care about every aspect of your personal life to keep it above reproach. If you're going to be stoned, be stoned for being a prophet, not for some trivial little mistake!" Any prophetic clergyperson takes risks.

But there are various ways to be a leader. A gifted speaker, called to a large congregation in the Midwest, knew that his interpretation of truth, administered forcefully, would arouse consternation among his new charges. He resolved to give only Bible study in his first year's sermons, with almost no reference to social issues. He also did an earnest job of becoming the people's pastor, visiting in their homes, praying with them, showing them what was the basis for his own understanding of the Word. Then, in his fifty-third week, he began to reveal what he honestly regarded as the social impact of his texts. The congregation was surprised, and at first alarmed. But by this time they knew him personally and trusted him. By first winning their respect as their pastor and teacher, he had prepared them for his also being a prophet in relation to social issues. His ministry became notably effective because he balanced all the roles of teacher, pastor, priest, and prophet.

This case is also an illustration of the fact that most members of a group look for integrity, authenticity, and courage in anyone who speaks a prophet's word. Prophets must stand unaccounted for by anything except the force and truth of what they find the Lord saying. If the congregation senses the sincerity of the clergyperson's prophetic message, it will be far more accepting of the teachings. Consider this final illustration: An elder went to another elder with a series of quotations from their leader's sermons, charging heresy and social radicalism in his theology. His colleague heard him out, and then said, "There's nothing wrong with that man's theology! Do you remember how last winter when my wife was sick he came here and stayed up all night with me at her bedside? There's nothing wrong with that man's ideas at all." Here again, the pastor side of a ministry served to balance the potentially harsher aspects of the prophet side.

There is an old saying that "Scripture doesn't say anything against tact." This is especially relevant in commending truth. The prophet is hardly called to be overly shrewd or conniving in giving the Word, but instead to present the religious beliefs as effectively and convincingly as possible.

Actual areas for prophecy among the clergy are not hard to find. Disarmament, world law, and justice offer innumerable occasions for prophetic commentary and action. The list of prophetic possibilities is virtually endless. Just some topics include racial prejudice, violence on television, coexistence of extreme wealth with poverty (and the indifference and greed that this implies), Bible illiteracy, care of AIDS sufferers, prison reform, rebuilding the family, abortion and birth control, and enlarging congregational giving to worthwhile causes. Again it is worth remarking that able, inspired, honest clergy can be the most powerful agents for social change anywhere around the globe.

How Clergy Live

To round out the general picture of the clergy at work, here are some additional observations:

• **Clergy members work harder.** A union official has marveled at what he calls "the self-exploitation of the clergy." He said that despite any scoffing that these men and women work for only an hour or two a week, his own experience for many years has been that the typical clergyperson overworks. Labor, he says, complains that managers and owners exploit it, while managers growl that they are victimized by labor. In the clergy, however, it is the workers themselves who do the exploiting! They never feel entirely at ease, he says, on the golf links or the tennis courts. They are always a bit fretful on summer vacation because time is going by and the world still needs being saved. They are reluctant, he says, to spend any single hour just having a good time.

This comment does not apply everywhere. As in any type of work, some clergypeople qualify as merely indolent timeservers and corner-cutters. Far more are undeniably workaholics. They put in many more hours per week than most other workers do. Are you lazy? If so, don't aim for ordination!

• **Clergy members live longer.** An Old Testament verse goes, "With long life will I satisfy Him, and show Him my salvation." Whether the latter part of this promise of the Lord is always fulfilled or not, certainly the first part is widely demonstrated among the clergy. In spite of their tendencies to overwork, they are durable indeed. Life insurance for clergy is notoriously cheaper than for nearly all other workers. Members of the clergy seem to live on and on! Is it because they eat less, drink less, smoke less, relieve their worries in prayer, and live contentedly? (Incidentally, the widows of male clergy, living on a pension, are even more long-lived. As one insurance man marveled, "They sometimes seem completely indestructible!")

In contrast to what advertisers flaunt as the good life (hectic luxury trips, self-indulgent personal habits, and opulent estates), the sturdy corps of the very old ministers of God testifies to a very different meaning of the term "good."

• **Clergy members are increasingly well paid.** One longtime tradition plaguing the leaders of congregations is that their income is appreciably less than that of other professions that make similar educational demands. Assuredly, the salaries of lawyers and physicians, and some teachers and educational administrators, are far in excess of clergy incomes. Also, many wage earners such as mechanics, plumbers, electricians, and assembly-line workers—even with high union dues, limited weekly schedules, and layoffs—receive paychecks that are bountiful in comparison. Priests are known to receive modest remuneration because they are celibate and thereby exempt from the expense of a family. Protestant clergy families proverbially have been assumed to live like church mice. Rabbis experience similar standards of living. Most people judge clergy to be at the low end of the income scale of the community.

Although this is still true for many, more recently it has become less rare, for clergy are better paid than many members of their congregations. With the rise in the cost of living, solicitous congregational committees have steadily upped salaries and expense arrangements for car, travel, and home. Most priests' allowances have also been increased. Such changes render obsolete a classic instance of the former way of reckoning clerical salaries. A businessman board member was horrified at the salary increase proposed for the pastor, and objected, "Why, he'd be getting almost as much as I do. That's absurd! His work is done for other kinds of reward."

Still, that standard sometimes persists in rural areas, fading congregations, the inner city, and in some missionary fields. The old practice of congregation members leaving a sack of potatoes, flour, or vegetables on the clergyperson's porch still lingers in some places. But with the minimums set in presbyteries, dioceses, conferences, and associations or synods, clerical salaries and expense arrangements nowadays are far above poverty levels. Besides, in the old tradition of plain living and high thinking, clerical households usually spend and save wisely, even in a prodigally high standard of living generation. No one should turn away from a career in religion just because it's assumed that it doesn't pay enough.

Most clergy members have retirement pensions. Here again there is a contrast between national mainline religious groups and small, independent congregations. Retirement provisions are, without exception, available for Catholic priests. Other major religious groups subsidize pension plans and retirement communities that are frequently more responsible than those offered to industrial or business employees. Clergy usually count on Social Security, for which they are of course eligible, to complement pension payments, which, it must be granted, are modest at most.

A growing custom among ministers and rabbis is the practice of buying a house instead of living in quarters furnished by the congregation. It is a far cry from the days when few clergy could afford a home or a summer cottage. Clergy, for better or for worse, are pretty solidly settled in middle-class habits.

• **Clergy members read more and keep learning.** It is well known in the publishing business that members of the clergy can be counted on to buy more books and periodicals than almost any other occupational group. For one thing, their business deals almost entirely in words. Television, movies, and the Internet tend to draw millions further and further from the traditionally printed communication of ideas. But those who preach, teach, and counsel still find many resources in printed materials. It is likely that the clergyperson's personal library is the largest in the neighborhood, partly because of the continuing need to search for new ideas and facts.

This same conscientiousness impels many members of the clergy to sign up for refresher courses, seminars, and retreats. Summer institutes for clergy of every tradition are often overcrowded with many listeners poised, notebook or computer on laps, for fresh insights or illustrations. They keep learning all their lives to deepen their effectiveness and exercise their obedience to God. In few other fields is this process so continuous and satisfying.

• **Clergy members are on an inward journey.** A large number of clergypeople find their occupation a deepening adventure and a personal pilgrimage. Thus, when a member of the clergy goes on a retreat (for a weekend, for an eight-day Ignatian withdrawal to a monastery or convent, or for a several-week experience of self-examination and gratitude to God), it is, in most cases, not to improve efficiency at the job or get new ideas, but to give one's self to God more fully and profoundly. Many clergy annually make a retreat of this sort and find themselves enlarged and lifted up by it. In some sense part of their professional self-improvement, it is in greater measure a personal venture into wholeness.

We have suggested that clergy activities drain a person if they are undertaken in deep sincerity. Sympathizing with a succession of tangled life stories, doing all the work a congregation involves, preparing presentations, and even interceding in prayer for people—it all makes demands that call for spiritual replenishment. This reinvigorating can for most leaders take place only in silence, contemplation, and waiting upon God. All of these are a privilege to the dedicated person, and it is a manifest blessing to be free to be spiritual and seek the Presence as part of one's life calling.

- **Clergy members usually have a satisfying group life among themselves.** Few professional gatherings are as rewarding to their members as those in the clergy. The area Council of Churches, with diverse representation from very dissimilar churches, is often an exercise in strategy, mutual deference, devotion to cooperation, and enjoyable levity. Gatherings with other clergy members of one's own communion or order can be a time for trading news of friends, meeting recently joined colleagues, sharing prayer, singing, and experiencing general satisfaction. Even committee meetings, in which shared knowledge of Scripture can prompt many an adroit bon mot or exchange of references, become a pleasing social occasion.

At the risk that clergy members may comprise a clergy class, or that their meeting together can become a time to share endless occupational small talk or to compete in piousness, face-to-face gatherings of clerical fellowship are extremely satisfying events. A veteran office secretary for a congregation declared, "Nobody has more enjoyment in just getting together than ministers and priests and rabbis. It must make them feel they are a sort of family of God when they realize they are joined together in His business."

- **Clerical households are often notable.** When Catholic clergy or monastics engage in informal discussion of whether priests should marry, a recurring point is always whether family life in the rectory, manse, or parsonage is really desirable, for either the family or the clergy. For some, spouses and children are a distraction from the essential ordained task. For many others, however, they bring a number of advantages.

It was once said that, "If you want to get into *Who's Who in America*, arrange to be born into the family of a clergyman." This was because, in the early years of that publication, it was said that a third of all the persons listed therein were from clerical backgrounds—a situation hardly prevailing today. But ministers' sons and daughters continue to be an interesting segment of the population. They are brought up in a home where there is a big library and where they are well educated and taught good manners. Frequently, they go on to ordination, like their fathers or mothers. Sometimes, in rebellion against their backgrounds, they become worst in every category in the neighborhood. One harried clergy parent, with her several children all seemingly in this last category, sighed that her family was a notable recommendation for the celibacy of the clergy! Clearly, it is not worth becoming ordained just to have children that are born into a clerical family. But the whole question of family life presents one of the special factors in considering a career in religious service.

4

SERVING AS A CHAPLAIN

A CHAPLAIN IS a clergyperson who is employed to serve the spiritual needs of a group that itself doesn't choose or employ this person. A chaplain is someone made available by a program or institution. Customarily, the chaplain's duties involve counseling, worship leadership, and relations with families of the group. The chaplain is generally expected to serve as the religious adviser of the whole program and its staff.

Hospital Chaplain

Most chaplains are in this job category. The hospital chaplain either may be part of the hospital's paid personnel or is sometimes sent in by a nearby Council of Churches or other community agency. In psychiatric institutions, general hospitals, and Veterans Administration hospitals, the chaplain typically has office hours from nine to five but spends most of the time visiting patients at their beds or in lounges, occasionally even being invited into an operating room (with appropriate mask and antiseptic garb). In addition to these duties, the chaplain also supervises seminarians receiving counseling training at the hospital. He or she leads their daily roundtable discussions and advises each of them personally.

Large hospitals have Protestant, Catholic, and Jewish chaplains, each with an office near the customary interdenominational chapel. All are regarded as members of the nonmedical staff. They regularly notify local clergy when members of their congregations are admitted, thus serving as the most active liaison person in the neighborhood. At times of grave crisis, they can be of notable help to patients and families. The services of worship that they lead for the patients may be crucial morale builders, and for Catholics, this includes serving Mass to all who ask for it. Sometimes the chaplain is the only person who can explain to the family or visitor, in nontechnical terms, the condition of a patient.

This is normally a temporary, crisis ministry. For most it is less satisfying than working with a congregation. It isolates an ordained woman or man among members of a different professional group, many of whom have little regular use for religion.

Yet the hospital chaplain's role is deeply rewarding for a clergyperson who is skillful in getting along with strangers, is interested in medical therapies, has preaching abilities adaptable to an institutional chapel, and has special concern for ministering to the whole person. In recent years there have been new strides toward this sort of holistic goal of dealing with a person's spirit, mind, and body as a unified entity. When chaplains genuinely know that their gifts in the healing of a patient can be as effective as are those of the physician, this becomes an exciting venture in faith.

Correctional Institution Chaplain

In a land where there are hundreds of thousands of prisoners, religious ministry to them is a dramatic necessity. State and federal penitentiaries, from minimum to maximum security; reformatories for men and for women; industrial schools for delinquents; youth development centers; and local jails and county prisons all usually have either a part-time or a full-time chaplain.

As in hospitals, the work of the clergyperson here takes place in an atmosphere far different from that of a parish or temple congregation. Tangible obstacles include fear, brutality, envy, greed, and despair. Clergy members or others who have an excess of sympathy, or a sentimental overidentification with the imprisoned, are ill-advised to consider such a ministry. One penitentiary warden, after commending the new chaplain as their best ever, shook his head and said: "But we're going to have to get rid of him, because he takes all nine hundred prisoners home every night and worries about them. He's getting an ulcer already. We all know you can't let these human situations get to you." The special quality of objectivity is needed for the chaplain in a correctional institution.

At the same time, the chaplain needs a durable eagerness to share spiritual resources with inmates and also with the correction officers who watch over them. Evangelizing, an old custom in prison preaching, is surely not recommended in its typical forms.

But it is essential that the clergyperson be ready to commend religious solutions to inmates' difficulties, not merely provide psychological analyses. Among younger offenders there is the added call for the chaplain's serving as a model, in lives where few if any have existed before. As the one person not completely a part of the establishment of the prison, the chaplain may be also the one who is able to offer a pattern for rehabilitation. Priest, pastor, or rabbi, the chaplain may be able to open spiritual doors in a closed world.

Military Chaplain

In the U.S. Army, Navy, Coast Guard, Air Force, and Marines, chaplains are far more in evidence during a war than during peaceful times. But the military, which can suddenly lift men and women out of home and community, is traditionally obliged to provide chaplains all of the time.

For some men and women, this may be a lifetime career. It offers security, a residence on the base, advances in rank, very early retirement, and lifelong pensions in addition to Veterans Administration benefits. The temptation here is to sink into serving in only a routine military way, waiting for retirement and hoping war does not come. Military rank, however, takes such mere timeserving into account. The up-or-out policy of the armed services ordinarily applies to all officers, and if a chaplain is twice passed over for promotion, he or she is normally discharged. Why? Speaking of all chaplains, the Catholic Chancellor of the Military Ordinariate once granted: "Sometimes you can find that a man is a fine priest but he just doesn't fit in with the military." There have been suggestions that the chaplain should have no rank at all, like a warrant officer, but this, too, could be a put-down in a rank-dominated system.

For short-term chaplains, this period of service is sometimes viewed as doing a military turn in a succession of positions in ministry. Even without valuable familiarity in the job, this pattern often brings forth a lot of vigor in chaplains. It makes the military a mission field for one assigned period. Such mobility also blunts the old criticism that it is a paradox for the government, devoted to separation of church and state, to employ clergy of particular faiths.

An ongoing need exists for chaplains, because many mainline religious groups cannot come up with enough personnel to fill their quotas. Each major denomination is asked to provide numbers according to a percentage-of-population scale, and this they often find they cannot do. In wartime, many conscientious clergy (sometimes even including avowed pacifists) find the chaplaincy an imperative duty. In peacetime, recruits are hard to find. Some years ago, Catholic chaplain ranks were well short of their quota, with more than half the empty places being in the Army. As these and other large communions fail to meet their quota, the intergroup Commission on Chaplains fills up the void from among candidates available in groups with more zeal, but often less education and training.

If there is to be a military chaplaincy at all (and everyone seems to find it a real need) then there should surely be enough men and women of high caliber to make the program a sturdy witness to Hebrew-Christian concerns. Chaplains themselves may even bring about new changes to ennoble and enlarge this needed ministry. We salute the considerable number of ordained clergy who strive to make the system work.

Campus Chaplain

Colleges, universities, and private schools offer chaplaincies that, compared with those in the military, are far less secure but decidedly more colorful. On denominationally affiliated campuses, there is regularly to be found a dean of the chapel, a campus pastor, or at the very least, a religious adviser. Some of these men and women think of such roles as a lifetime occupation on the same campus, becoming significant parts of campus life as the decades roll by. Others in the same role may prefer a short-term stint as an assistant chaplain or staff member. Still others find satisfaction in an appointed pastorate for one or more denominational families of students.

Special ministries among American students are more than a century old. First came the YMCA and YWCA and a global-view missionary thrust called the Student Volunteer Movement, whose motto was "The world for Christ in this generation!" There were as yet few campus ministries for Catholics and Jews. At campus rallies, emancipated students began to make scathing appraisals of what their congregations back home did or did not do. Partly in response to such criticism, the major denominations themselves decided to gather their own constituents on campus, with religious centers and chaplains.

The first such center was the Jewish Hillel Foundation house at the University of Illinois. Soon costly denominational facilities sprang up at hundreds of campuses. Examples included the Newman Club for Catholics, Canterbury for Episcopalians, Wesley for Methodists, Westminster for Presbyterians, the Lutheran Student Association, Roger Williams or Baptist Student Union for Baptists, LDS for Mormons, UCC for United Church of Christ students, and many more. For a large university, even the weekly staff gathering of these chaplains became a roomful of congenial men and women. It still occurs on many campuses.

But since the middle of the last century, there has been a marked decline in the number of campus workers paid by national agencies. Returning World War II veterans were somehow not caught up by the YMCA, YWCA, and these denominational groups that formed a National Intercollegiate Christian Council with thousands of student members. Instead, the schools themselves began to appoint religious advisers, chaplains, and—as has been mentioned—hundreds of classroom professors of religion. Religion was no longer sandwiches and tea at Sunday evening discussions, or a home away from home. Now it became a classroom course with assignments and exams.

Meanwhile, nonadministrative movements, avowedly nonsectarian, began to send their chaplains in large numbers to work with students. These groups included Inter-Varsity Christian Fellowship, Campus Crusade for Christ, F.C.A. (the Fellowship of Christian Athletes), Catholic charismatic groups, and even Jews for Jesus. Huge national student assemblies began to rival in popularity the Student Volunteer conventions of the previous student generation.

Who can be an effective chaplain in the sometimes fast-moving campus arena? Although colleges are often thought of as being antireligious in sympathy, many actually support a wide range of religious thought. To be appointed dean of the chapel or a staff person to be pastor among Catholic, Jewish, or Protestant groups offers a tantalizing experience, even though perhaps a rough one.

Qualifying for such jobs requires seminary training, including courses dealing with student interests, if possible. The best recommendation for this work is to have been active yourself in an undergraduate program or in a congregation that was affiliated with a school.

Some university clergypeople, in later years, settle back into the less-demanding premises of the private or public high school. Campus tasks can be envisaged as a lifelong career or a short-term, colorful one. Whichever, they will continue (under denominational or administrative or free-movement auspices) to be crucial to the religious growth of America, her students, and the world.

5

TEACHING RELIGION

CHAPTER 3 DEALT with some aspects of what clergy members do as teachers in carrying out their duties in a parish or temple. As has been emphasized, no part of their work is more important in upholding and exploring religious faith.

For others, the desire to teach children, youth, and adults may not be related to clerical roles, but be involved with classrooms, textbooks, and the rewards of observing growth in learning. Not all of us have experienced the situations in which an ordained person does her or his work, but all of us have had contacts with the classroom. For the most part, we find the image of the instructor attractive and worthwhile. Many thousands of Americans have invoked at one time or another the words of an old Sunday school or catechism teacher. Teachers of religion, especially during our impressionable years, occupy a strategic position in the shaping of our religious ideas and behavior.

In this discussion we'll be concerned only with the paid, professional teacher, not the volunteer. In America, there are many thousands of such full-time instructors in religion. In the earlier grades, most of these are in Catholic parochial schools and parish catechism centers, with a growing number of personnel in religious day schools at that level. For high school and college students, the proportion of Protestant and Jewish instructors is much greater. According to the Center for Education Reform, nearly seven thousand Catholic elementary schools are now in operation in the United States, along with more than twelve hundred secondary schools. All of these schools represent employment possibilities for qualified faculty.

Teaching in the Primary Grades

For more than one hundred years, Americans have been accustomed to having women teachers be almost solely responsible for education in the elementary grades. This is a practice that developed during the nineteenth century, when tax-supported public education entered our national picture. Before that, the schoolmaster was almost always a man, and usually a clergyman.

More recently, there has been a movement to employ more men in teaching children in the public schools. In countless one-parent families, it has been found that many children have no contact with a man, week after week. To balance their experiences in such fatherless households, the male schoolteacher is an important element in children's growth. As this same condition is dealt with in Catholic elementary grades, Hebrew schools, and Christian day schools (mostly with an evangelical, conservative stamp), men teachers can be confident of the increasing employment opportunities.

Critical of what they regard as mediocrity in the public school system, various educational philosophers have founded other schools in dozens of cities in the United States and Canada. Montessori schools (the first of which began in Rome in 1907) teach preschool children initiative, sharper sense perception, and coordination in an atmosphere friendly to religion. Waldorf schools, based on the ideas of Rudolf Steiner (1861–1925), emphasize non-competition among children and the belief that by certain kinds of self-discipline we may know the spiritual world directly. Alongside these systems, religious day schools provide less educational theory but more zeal. State-run institutions for children with special needs or disabilities are often particularly receptive to teachers who have religious motivation, but who are willing to skip explicit instruction in religion.

It is worthwhile to mention that in a great number of tax-supported public schools at the elementary level, religious teachers have found a real vocation, without giving explicit religious training. By their sympathy, nonviolence, and personal concern for their pupils—and among teacher colleagues with less religious motivation—they can be effective spiritually, much as they would in a religious school. That is, all teaching of religion is certainly not done only in religious schools.

A way in which a number of men and women have entered primary-level education in religion is through writing educational materials for teaching. Translating profound ideas for small children, in words and pictures, is an important gift.

Teaching in High School, Day School, and Boarding School

The offering of released-time religion classes on certain days of the week, either in the public school building or nearby places of worship, is an arrangement worked out in many American cities. This is an option students and their parents may choose or reject. For several hours each week the teacher of religion offers, for diploma credits toward graduation, courses in the Bible and religious history and doctrine. Catholic students in some cases go to the nearby catechism center for such instruction.

In many American suburbs, full-time private day schools operate with the public educational program, often offering classes in religion. Sometimes under the guidance of a particular religious group, but more often operated under a board made up of parents and contributors, such independent schools train thousands of students eager to get into good colleges. A down-to-earth teacher of religion in these institutions is in a position to influence many prospective leaders of the community. Many are Catholic schools, as previously noted. Hebrew schools, located downtown or in suburbs, sometimes offer a full-scale high school curriculum, but usually are more like the released-time programs operated in conjunction with public high schools. Anyone privileged to teach teenagers in any of these programs knows how alert and critical students during these years can be as they look at religion. It is a challenging occupation, to say the least.

Fewer placements are available in boarding schools than in day schools, but teaching of religion there is often an even more important part of the curriculum. An instructor who is on the campus day and night has an opportunity to develop a serious attitude toward religion among the resident students and members of the faculty. The family and the household can be a living example. Even if economic realities during the coming decades close down many boarding schools, those that remain will continue to offer important opportunities for the teaching of religion. Distinguished Catholic boarding schools, others oriented to formal Episcopalian worship, and others with liberal or conservative religious traditions will maintain a pivotal position in training tomorrow's leaders. First-rate teachers are in demand to interpret spiritual values and truths in these special situations.

Teaching in Colleges and Universities

Until the middle of the twentieth century, religion was taught in most private and all church-affiliated colleges, but not in tax-supported state colleges and universities. The same constitutional provision against any establishment of religion, which separates public schools from parochial schools, obviously applied here. Tax-supported campuses had to depend on nearby places of worship and on the voluntary student programs that brought religion to the area. The YMCA and YWCA took wide responsibility in organizing and staffing undergraduate religious life. Through the developments of chaplaincies, the institutions themselves began to take a part in the teaching of religion, especially after the mid-twentieth century.

Particularly when veterans returned from World War II, with the G.I. Bill of Rights enabling them to take free college instruction, there was a new demand for religion courses at the undergraduate level. The effectiveness of volunteer religious groups eroded on campuses during the war, but upon their return, veterans asked for studies that would round out the whole curriculum they wanted. Tax-supported schools found that the constitutional restrictions on religious instruction and enforced faith did not prevent teaching about religion, if taught as any other subject. So within a decade, hundreds of teachers of religion were employed in tax-supported colleges as never before. Departments of religion came into being where the whole idea of them would have been laughed at just a few years before. Religion as an objective study, not a matter of belief, came to the campus to stay.

The formula thus developed was in many ways a strange one. It called for professors of religion who would present their subject matter in a completely impartial, dispassionate manner. Preachers had always asked for commitment to what they were declaring. Men and women teaching religion in church-affiliated colleges had always assumed that their listeners at least nominally subscribed to the theological doctrines represented by the institution. But now the call was for teachers who were in many respects prohibited from indicating where they stood in relation to the sacred claims they described in class. In no other area of university academic work is it so important to know where the instructor personally takes his or her position. Should we appoint teachers to explore a subject that they themselves don't essentially care about?

This dilemma, between preaching in class or indicating that "I couldn't care less," has been solved by most religion professors with an introductory avowal of their own background of belief and then the pledge to be as impartial as they can in describing their own and other religions. At one college, the professor of comparative religion was so convincing as she described each world faith, that the course was nicknamed the God-of-the-Month class! Yet the insistence on most campuses is that teachers must inform without proselytizing.

Compared with other academic levels discussed in this book, teaching religion in college is considerably more complicated. As students come to class, they may have just emerged from a physics class, where they had been learning about the laws of motion or the makeup of the atom. Or they may have had a philosophy course that directly seeks to debunk all theism. To be a gladiator for the faith in an arena that, by its very nature, challenges various notions demands an excellent mind, a vast inventory of facts, lively courage, and endless ingenuity. Even in religious-affiliated colleges, professors of religion may find themselves continually on the defensive.

Indeed, there are many different religions of the world, and they are all equally explored in higher institutions of learning. For example, Muslims make up one of the larger religious groups in North America. Like Christianity, Islam is the worship of only one God; Muhammad is His prophet. Among other world religions are Hinduism, Buddhism, and the Chinese religions of Confucianism and Taoism.

Thus the practice of teaching religion in colleges, if it genuinely involves both teaching and religion, asks for the best brains and dispositions available. When the Hebrew and Christian faiths, confronting all the forces of secularism in the academic establishment, call for a brilliant, convincing, and disciplined presentation of their intellectual and spiritual cores, it is from professors of religion that this presentation must come. Those involved in graduate teaching and research are asked for even greater wisdom and deeper conviction.

Educational Preparation

A majority of those who teach religion in schools and colleges are ordained clergy or members of religious orders, which means that they have fulfilled the educational requirements for that status. This has meant college and seminary for many, or special religious study.

Anyone looking forward to teaching religion in a public or private high school, day school, or boarding school, is well advised to attend college for the regular teacher's certificate granted by the state. Since this is usually not available in the field of religion, it can be earned in any teaching area, as a sign that the recipient is of teacher caliber. It also means that the graduate has taken education courses and has most likely spent some time student teaching, both of which are useful to the religion teacher. Instructors in programs of released-time religious instruction, who are not parish or temple staff members, particularly need this certification. Going on for a master's degree—either in religion at a theological school, or in education—is advantageous also.

For college teaching preparation, a master's degree in religion is almost certainly needed. Admission to a master's degree program requires a successful undergraduate career, with both grades and standardized test scores serving as criteria for evaluation. It is preferable to take this graduate work at a seminary or theological graduate school, partly just to share the preordination atmosphere and serious commitment there. Ordinarily, completion of the requirements for the master's degree takes one to two years of full-time study, sometimes more. It also serves to link the student to a particular religious group: Catholic, Lutheran, Methodist, Jewish, Presbyterian, Baptist, and so on. In some cases, this identification with the denomination to be served is mandatory, for one school year at least. It also provides one with a particular theological direction rather than a bland acceptance of all the religious alternatives. Religion comes not in bulk but only in brands. One must be identified with one tradition or denomination, not all of them.

The highest degree in religious study, as in any academic field, is the doctorate. This can be the doctor of philosophy degree (Ph.D.) or other doctoral degree. Sooner or later, any person teaching at a college or university must get this degree to remain on the job or receive a promotion. Seminaries and some universities award a doctor of theology or a doctor of sacred theology degree, but the

Ph.D. tends to be the most prestigious degree for teaching and research. The seminary degree, involving three years of study usually leading to ordination, is the master's in divinity (M.Div.). Along the same ministerial lines, the doctor of ministry (D.Min.), represents further work done after several years served in the clergy, although only a limited number of seminaries grant it.

How long do these courses of study take? As is well known, a bachelor's degree generally requires four years of study, although many students take longer. The master's degree may take one to three years beyond that, followed by several more years for a Ph.D. or other terminal degree. At some universities, the master's is awarded for two years' residence study, with rather demanding exams at the end of this period. After that, an acceptable dissertation, which is a book-length thesis in a very specialized field, qualifies one (after passing oral exams about the written tome) for the Ph.D. You might think there's no end to the academic grind necessary to prepare for teaching religion! Normally it adds up to about eleven years after high school—approximately the same time required of Catholics qualifying for ordination to the priesthood. For many candidates in such academic programs, the testing process measures eagerness, endurance, and patience as much as it measures the quantity of facts remembered and the sharpness of intellect acquired.

Is the training required for upper-level teaching a hurdle that a candidate reading this book may find altogether too high? Will it cost too much? For the person guided by high intention, every year of it can be an adventure and a delight. The person exhilarated by learning is also likely to be exhilarated by teaching.

6

MISSIONARY ROLES

HISTORICALLY, MANY CATHOLICS and Protestants have been daring, creative missionaries seeking both to spread the word of their faith and to help others. Although Jews have not had such a tendency to travel the world converting others, today Zionism and other return-to-Israel movements possess such a character. In this chapter we will discuss what it means to establish a religious service career as a missionary.

International Service

The word *missionary* comes from the Latin *missi*, which simply means "those sent." Our military use of the term, as in "sent on a mission," also has a task-force emphasis, indicating that a group goes somewhere to do something.

Today the approach of missions is significantly different than it once was, which was essentially the desire to tame "savage" cultures. We are now aware that all cultures are important and have much to teach those not familiar with their norms, values, and beliefs and that, as human beings, we are all members of one global family. Consequently, missionary strategy is actually the process of deploying anywhere in the world the task forces people need there to help them resolve some problem. It may mean missions from Angola to Argentina and from Pakistan to Peru. It is not unusual to meet enthusiastic Mormon (Church of Jesus Christ of Latter-Day Saints) missionaries, young men on their two-year stint to tell others about their faith, in Rome, Edinburgh, or Melbourne. But this long-distance travel is what an aggressive missionary policy can mean. Service Committee youth sent by the Church of the Brethren or the Mennonites to share agricultural experience with farmers in developing countries are empowered by the same world-minded spirit. In forms both old and new, such mission is the life of vital religion.

Perhaps no aspect of global life has an appeal so picturesque and dramatic. Religious mission has a rich heritage of pioneers, martyrs, doctors, literacy experts, heroic explorers, and saints. Before plane travel, remoteness and rugged existence at many mission stations made missions a task for only the toughest and most deeply convinced. Today the hazards are really just as grueling, but perhaps in different ways.

Today, missions are seldom found on inaccessible mountain peaks or among voracious cannibals. Rather, they call from American ghettos, from among terrorists abroad, and in countries ruled by hostile governments. Many citizens of other nations sit at their color TV sets and yearn for convenience foods, cola drinks or stronger ones, and electronic gadgets, not the intangible salvation of one hundred years ago. So, on the plane going overseas, today's missionary sits beside the Pepsi salesman, the seller of American baby foods or Chevrolets, and the World Bank loan executive. Each is being sent, but on very different missions.

In recent decades, there has been massive criticism of all overseas missions, both Protestant and Catholic, because many believed that overzealous missionaries were disturbing other cultures' religious traditions. In addition, many believed that, in Africa and Latin America especially, missions have failed. Rebel leaders, the story goes, have all actually been trained in mission schools (where they got, in fact, revolutionary ideas of freedom and the know-how to obtain it). Opponents of missions have cried out that it is precisely in lands where billions of American dollars have been spent that terrorism, government torture, and ruthless denial of human rights have become commonplace.

As a result of this negative press, mission-giving in this country has seriously declined, among both Protestants and Catholics. Overseas staffs have been cut again and again. Missionaries, once housed in comfortable settings, now usually share extremely modest quarters. Hospitals and schools built and staffed with mission funds have, partly by original intention, been turned over to local government agencies. After decades in which mission boards in this country asked Americans for undesignated giving, there has been a return to giving to this or that specific project, by congregations and concerned donors.

Despite such cutbacks in the number sent by the big denominations each year to missions abroad or in our own country, there continues a steady stream of persons, young and old, who become missionaries. Most bring specialized skills to their tasks. They include nurses, doctors, teachers, veterinarians, literary experts, recreation directors, agronomists, engineers, business machines technicians, child-care specialists, theology professors, and street preachers. When a married couple goes, or two nuns or two priests, they often have complementary skills, such as expertness in soil chemistry and teaching English. Salaries are steady, but by no means luxurious. Schooling, travel, medical and dental needs, and retirement plans are ordinarily taken care of.

In addition to Catholic and Protestant mission agencies, other types of faith organizations send personnel abroad from the United States and Canada. Funds to send these are typically raised by radio and television appeals. Unfortunately, official groups and overseas governments often regard the work of missionaries as old-fashioned emotional evangelism, and they often fail to note that, increasingly, it involves expert service by trained specialists.

The designation "faith missions" has meant that if funds do come in, salaries are paid; if they do not, workers abroad are left stranded without income, often moving in at nearby regular mission stations until the home treasury is replenished. Established mission boards and the Catholic orders have long objected, mildly, that it takes quite as much faith to set up a year's budget in advance as it does to raise the money. But regardless of an uncertain salary, many candidates for mission service prefer to be commissioned by the faith enterprises.

Missions in North America

To be sent for task work in North America is quite as clearly a missionary program as being sent to the ends of the earth—less glamorous, perhaps, but of as great a need. Such efforts serve Native Americans; Hispanic Americans; migrant workers; immigrant Koreans, Vietnamese, and Haitians; and other disadvantaged groups.

Here, one aim is the same as that of overseas missions: the task of the missionary is to work himself or herself out of a job by helping to build up leadership locally. Home mission projects can include hinterland hospitals, old-age facilities, language schools, craft centers, settlement houses in blighted neighborhoods, rescue missions in disadvantaged neighborhoods, child-care programs and vaccination clinics, motherhood-training classes, summer camps for children or families, sickle-cell anemia clinics, adobe house-building projects, Alcoholics Anonymous chapters, credit unions for young people—the list of mission concerns in North America for all religious denominations is incredibly long and varied.

One of the most ingenious mission efforts carried on for many years now is the Christian Ministry in National Parks. This program delegates several hundred seminarians each summer to serve as hotel employees in our national parks. They are paid like the other workers but equipped to lead worship services on Sunday, to counsel with other students on the workforce, and to help interpret wilderness majesty as God's own creation. Participants are told to announce worship not in some narrow chapel, but right out beside, for example, the Yosemite Falls cataract. In winter, other seminarians or furloughed pastors become (with the cooperation of the management) chaplains at ski resorts, offering prayer and song at the beginning point of the ski run. In a land where most areas of religious endeavor have burned out, such deft, inspired kinds of home missions demand courage and infinite creativity of the young missionaries.

Is such a missionary task attractive to you? Often it is not so well paid as a suburban parish job could be. It is less glamorous than much overseas work, and one cannot return from Idaho able to say good morning to the church school or catechism center in Swahili! For married people, raising a family among the less privileged is difficult as these areas typically have substandard school systems and poor access to health care and other resources. There are formidable pitfalls and victories in North American missionary tasks.

The taunt comes from overseas that "Americans should clean up their own backyard first." It makes sense. But global missions cannot wait for America to become perfect before help is sent to friends abroad.

So here, too, a candidate for a career in religion must decide where he or she fits into the urgent program of sharing all our religious resources everywhere in the world. Jobs commissioned with the official mission agencies are significant, just as are those under free-moving, independent organizations. Wherever it goes or comes from, as thousands of dedicated mission workers testify, mission work is desperately urgent, timely, and imperative in our world history.

7

Religious Education and Music Careers

A PERSON WHO is knowledgeable in religious education or talented in religious music can anticipate a satisfying career in American congregations. Take a closer look at two positions in particular: director of religious education and director of music. Trained leaders in both areas play vital roles in the life of the congregation.

Director of Religious Education

In several thousand temples and churches in North America, a key staff member is the director of religious education. In regard to most religious occupations, Protestants and Catholics share more common concerns than they do with Jewish workers. But the profession of director of religious education is just the reverse: in Protestant and Jewish circles, the term "director of religious education" suggests an interfaith practice that is not a part of Catholic parishes. Protestant and Jewish directors of religious education, without the help of Catholic nuns or monks or catechism centers, tackle their jobs with a similar set of directives.

The director of religious education is the staff person who plans and directs teaching programs. Duties may include training volunteer or paid teachers, helping choose published materials to be used in the classroom, hiring teachers and superintendents, organizing the vacation school, cooperating with nearby public schools, setting up an adult laity school for weeknights, or gathering the youth groups for a wiener roast or prayer circle.

Very often employed by the governing committee of the temple or church, rather than personally by the clergy, the director of religious education wields authority vital to the well-being of the entire congregation. An observer of the witness and follow-through in a large congregation mused that "our director of religious education is far more influential in the development of children and youth here than are the clergypeople. Clergy come and go and are busy with preaching, calling, and serving the adults. It is the director of religious education who really affects the growth of young people in this community." This comment accurately describes the strategic importance of this task in congregations where such a staff person can be afforded.

Sometimes the director of religious education does have a lonely, and often unappreciated, job. The heroic image of the clergy—"Reverend, your sermon was just terrific today!"—is usually lacking for them. Teachers may disappoint them. Children may fail to improve. Worship climaxes may sometimes collapse. The clergy may neglect to commend them. Mothers may call to say their children were passed over for parts in the play. The ordered materials may arrive too late to be used.

On the other hand, the director of religious education who knows that he or she has a calling for this work, and who can pray for and with fellow workers, can be sure of lasting satisfaction. As the ordination of women has become more usual, many a director has completed additional study to take that step also. Yet the ablest in this job field need seek no added prestige or recognition: they find their vocation here deeply authentic and rewarding.

How do you prepare for this occupation? Paths vary. The director of religious education is sometimes a person with no specialized training or even a college degree. In other cases, he or she may have at least that credential, plus either seminary or graduate work. In planning a college program, it is logical for the candidate to take as many courses in religion as are available. Earning a teaching certificate is also helpful, since the worker with the congregation often has dealings with other educators in the area and may need this badge of office.

At many seminaries, the master's in religious education (M.R.E.) degree is particularly designed for students working in (or planning to work in) this occupational group. Usually it is a two-year degree. A master's in art or teaching is sometimes the alternative, with little difference in requirements. The courses normally include Scripture exegesis (critical interpretation of the Scriptures), along with the history of the gathered tradition and study of educational psychology. Field education duties are customarily added to the class work.

In the 1930s through the 1960s, there was substantial growth in religious education as a field of study. It was a popular major for both women and men. As time passed, this high expectation waned. More recently, many religious education professors and majors have complained that their specialty has been downgraded and underemphasized.

At the same time, new interest and renewed enthusiasm can be found in the area of religious education in some denominations, aided by growth in membership, new approaches to Bible study, and the use of multimedia resources. In many ways, the director of religious education still has a crucial task in contemporary culture.

Director of Music

Regardless of time or location, music has always been part of religious worship. What would worship and the individual's religious experience be without music? Think of just some of the examples: drum beats in traditional African religions, chants and oboe melodies in Asian temples, plainsong and the cantor in Jewish and Christian history, hymns and anthems, mountain choruses, guitar-led ballads, gospel songs with trumpets and tubas, or delicate motet choirs in churches and synagogues. When anyone with musical talent and training begins to feel enthused about the importance of melody and singing in the practice of his or her religion, the idea of being a director of music for a congregation may march right behind. Indeed, many people training to be professional musicians aim for the field of religious music as the core of meaning for all the time and effort expended. When the joyful sound—familiar in every rock group or bluegrass music festival—becomes something spiritually moving, it gathers new depth and importance.

The breadth of choice in music for congregations is wide indeed, involving organists, choir directors, cantors, soloists, revival song-leaders, handbell instructors, carillonneurs, teachers of children's songs, guitarists, pageant directors, blowers of the shofar for Hebrew services, members of string ensembles, and electronic-music experts. If you specialize in some other sort of music-making, chances are that it, too, is surely used somewhere in worship.

Except in large congregations, the job of the musician is normally to provide music for one or two worship services per week. This is part-time work, and even though there may be enjoyment in the task, the pay is often meager. An old saying is that the small amateur choir is often "the war department of the congregation," but actually it is more likely to be the weekly gathering of the most faithful core of the whole membership. Too seldom is the organist-choirmaster honored for being very important in the life of the group.

It is in the large congregation that the director of music is more likely to be a full-fledged, adequately paid professional. One role may be serving as the organist, but the whole program of music calls for the training of the adult and youth choirs. Aid to the clergy in choosing hymns and forms of liturgy is often expected. Actual education in music for the congregation may be provided as well. Brass bands are not unknown in large places of worship. Motet choirs and a cappella circles, jazz combos, and huge choruses are also part of the great variety. One director of music complained that he had to climb 103 steps in the campanile tower to play the thirty-ton chimes, and then hurry down to the lower basement to drill eight-year-olds with tiny brass bells in hand!

Many colleges and universities offer a major in religious music as part of a bachelor of arts (B.A.) degree. At the graduate level, several degrees are available with specialization in church and temple music: the master of fine arts (M.F.A.), master of sacred music (M.S.M.), and beyond these the doctor of sacred music (D.S.M.), which is offered at a few schools. When a musician in this field also puts after his or her name an A.G.O., it denotes membership in the American Guild of Organists, whereas an F.A.G.O. denotes being a Fellow of that Guild, an awarded distinction that involves a qualifying organ recital.

As an example of an undergraduate program, students at Appalachian State University in Boone, North Carolina, may pursue a bachelor's degree in sacred music that prepares them for full-time or part-time positions in church music. The program provides a foundation in understanding worship traditions and trends and also covers practical skills such as conducting, accompanying, performing, and working in administration.

Courses offered in this program include the following:

Liturgies and Hymnody
Organization and Philosophy of Church Music
Internship in Church Music
Service Playing (for keyboardists only)
Pedagogy and Literature (for all other students)

In addition, students complete the standard requirements taken by most music majors in areas such as music theory and aural skills, music history and literature, and conducting. Sacred music majors also complete some courses in music education.

At the Boston University School of Theology, students may earn a master of sacred music degree by completing a series of required courses in three categories: theology, music, and the ministry of music. To earn the degree, students must successfully complete sixty credit hours and a final project. The program includes theology requirements as well as those in music. Along with several other requirements, students participate in a Boston University music organization.

At Luther Seminary in St. Paul, Minnesota, a master of sacred music degree is offered in cooperation with St. Olaf College. The degree program provides an ecumenical focus within a Lutheran context. Available courses include (but are not limited to) the following:

Bible
Worship in Israel
History of Christianity
Christian History from the New Testament to the Present
Overview of Christian Teachings
Church Music
Ecumenical Hymnody
Applied Organ
Choral Conducting
Advanced Conducting
Applied Voice
Choral Literature
Applied Instrumental Study
Composing and Arranging for the Church (voices,
    instruments, handbells)
Children's Choir Repertoire and Technique

For anyone interested in this professional career, it is wise to consider both the surface and the deeper approaches to music in religion. The deeper angle may equip the director of music to interpret publicly pieces to be sung or played, with a word about their history, the intention of the composer, and the motives of the writer. The ability and desire to do this may reach back to the musician's own college courses in religion and music. Particular skills also may enable a director to teach in a nearby school or college, take on a radio hour, or sometimes offer individual lessons to choir members and others who take part in the congregation's music program. Many musicians in churches and temples are ordained clergypeople as well. This combination is a real find for a large congregation. Even those who attend just for the music may be unaware that this joyful music is actually musical preaching being done by a priest, rabbi, or minister.

8

Religious Administration and Social Work

For most of us, it is difficult to pinpoint far in advance the precise occupational spot we would like to have. As previously suggested, a variety of circumstances can occur during a person's lifetime to change the course of his or her vocation; often, these have more to do with a person's life odyssey than deliberate planning does. But it is fitting to take a look now at some jobs that are outside any of the categories of careers in religion that have thus far been discussed.

One is that of the ecumenical or interfaith executive. Another is the religious social worker, who also usually operates on an interfaith basis. In a time when many people are less and less denominational in their concerns, when many projects are being merged or made cooperative, and when serious and astute management in religious programs is needed, these two specializations are particularly relevant.

Administration

The religious bureaucrat is an essential functionary. This role may mean serving as an administrator or executive in a Catholic archdiocese or in the headquarters of the American Hebrew Congregation, the Council of Churches, the Church Federation, or a wide selection of interfaith agencies.

Sometimes, a student or practicing clergyperson senses from the beginning a calling to this kind of work and climbs toward it with determination. More often, the person who in a local project does a competent job is advanced to upper levels of management. Emerson suggested that if someone builds a better mousetrap, "the world will beat a path to his door."

It is perennially true that local workers need help and encouragement. And no one can provide this support effectively except somebody who knows other people's problems from within. So, executive work in religion can use, as preparation, any experience and training an individual has in dealing with people and operating a shared venture.

A wise executive remarked that a local worker who leaves that task with relief, liberated to do big things, is frequently found to be ineffective. By contrast, one who hates to leave the local projects and would really prefer to stay there, often does exceptionally well further up the line. Frequently the most capable candidates are also the most surprised at being exalted to a higher office.

For the most part, for good or ill, American religious organizations are patterned after the same model as American corporations.

Looking far back into history, some scholars have found that the very roots of capitalism began in the giant monastic orders of the Middle Ages with their widespread farms, granaries, ships, paid workers, and sense of business practicality. The chain of command needed to operate these large businesses was readily available in monastic life, too. Thus, when at the time of the Renaissance a new society reached for merchant-empire models, this was the pattern that best served its purposes. In some ways, organized church life calls for the same corporate structure.

When young people visit the bureaucratic headquarters of their religious organization, they are likely to object, "Is all this executive chain of command necessary? Do we really need archdeacons, presbytery executives, district superintendents, diocesan and chancellery officials, bishops, moderators, board secretaries, and conference brass?" One answer to such a yearning for simplicity and open fellowship is that to perform its service nationwide and worldwide, the religious organization has to be set up like any other international enterprise.

Some years ago, a foundation-funded Church Executive Development Board set out to train religious leaders for such responsibilities, rightly claiming that under these men and women several billion dollars are spent yearly, thousands of employees are hired, and critically important decisions are made. American industry invests in exhaustive screening, psychological and occupational testing, and skills training for its administrators. Their counterparts in the religious field must be no less expert and responsible.

Thus, the person who finds this aspect of the whole religious effort attractive is to be encouraged to prepare for administrative and executive duties in church or temple. Even though persons in this area find it useful to be prepared to do preaching, counseling, and other clerical tasks, these may be secondary considerations in seeking the most relevant type of ministry for the years ahead.

Let's look briefly at activities that fall within this administrative classification.

Councils of Churches

The Council of Churches movement, which began to gather strength in the first decades of the twentieth century, has since then been the major effort in cooperation among churches and temples. In many cities and towns, it took the place of the Ministerial Association, or Ministerium, which was a friendly seminar of religious leaders in the area.

The global counterpart of this movement has been the World Council of Churches, formed in Amsterdam, Holland, in 1948 and comprising 150 to 200 communions from dozens of countries. In general, the basis of membership has been a formula, variously revised, which says that these are bodies that "accept Jesus Christ as Lord." The council has its headquarters in an imposing skyscraper building (which it owns) in Geneva, Switzerland. With an assembly every several years, the council serves as the unified voice of Protestant and Orthodox groups and has relationships with the Catholic headquarters at the Vatican and with Orthodox headquarters as well. Often focusing on the interests of Third World countries, the World Council of Churches receives grants for its budget from member groups and offers help at various points of need around the world.

Although Jewish membership is often typical in town and city Councils of Churches, where leaders gather in face-to-face concern for their communities, there is no representation of Judaism in the National Council or the World Council of Churches. Consultation is frequent, however, with Jewish, Catholic, and other groups. The Unitarian Universalist denomination, which is described as non-creedal, and such movements as the Ethical Culture Society, are also in occasional communication.

Area Councils of Churches perform a variety of functions. They may coordinate union services among congregations; link Protestant and Catholic programs of social service; promote revival movements; express religious viewpoints about current issues; help to plan the placing of new congregations; push campaigns to adopt immigrants or deal with emergencies; or provide chaplains in prisons, hospitals, and orphanages. Opportunities to speak are plentiful. There is customarily an executive secretary, with an office staff and sometimes a small circle of subexecutives for special concerns. Salaries are modest, but travel allowances may be necessarily large.

Other Cooperative Religious Agencies

Other ecumenical or interfaith agencies often have positions similar to those of the Councils of Churches. Examples include the Catholic Peace Fellowship (which has headquarters in Notre Dame, Indiana) and the Jewish Peace Fellowship (with headquarters in Nyack, New York). Such groups, which promote peace and anti-militarism, may champion the cause of peace though measures such as sending out speakers and sponsoring conferences, seminars, and demonstrations. To carry out such work, these and other such groups may employ professional staff members.

Groups such as the Young Men's Christian Association (YMCA), Young Women's Christian Association (YWCA), and Jewish Community Centers of North America tended to be more explicitly religious at their founding than they are now. But in some strategic program spots in all three national movements, and also in local or area programs, people with a deep religious sense of calling make a real witness. In the worldwide effort to secure full civil rights for women, the YWCA has had a genuinely crucial impact. A recently graduated woman seminarian declared that she was not in the least interested in the parish or any "domestic" work (in either meaning of that term!), but was heading into the worldwide program of the YWCA, because she found it in many countries to be the one, single, influential force for the rights of women.

The YMCA also has a global outreach, and a number of jobs in its programs in America qualify as careers in religion. Counselors, youth program directors, summer camp executives and chaplains, Bible breakfast organizers at metropolitan YMCAs, and other similar positions are available. Usually YMCA activities are building-centered. Some years ago when the American YMCA raised millions of dollars in a worldwide "Buildings for Brotherhood" campaign, it was often pointed out that this is the typical American concern—buildings, brick, and mortar. Other YMCAs around the world carry on many of their programs with almost no buildings at all in many places, as they are more educationally and spiritually oriented and think less of swimming pools and gymnasiums.

Religious Social Work

In cities and towns across Canada, the United States, and abroad, and on the staffs of hundreds of parishes and temples are persons trained in social work who prefer to do it under religious auspices. This is a special occupation. Such religious social workers may come from the religious side in their training and interest, or from the social side.

Here again, although the sponsoring agency is usually a denominational one, the people served are from all sorts of backgrounds, religious or even antireligious. The center, sometimes called a settlement house, may be in the inner city. It may have gratings over its windows and heavy locks on its doors, a much-used gym with showers, meeting rooms, a kitchen, and several offices. The religious social worker here carries on amidst the yells of basketball players, the cacophony of children making music upstairs, the boisterous sounds at the mother's meeting, the tots playing tag in the hall, or the director interviewing the troublemaker or the glowing scholarship applicant in the front office. This can be seen as an effort to provide religion for the masses. Children and adults who darken the door of no church or synagogue come here for recreation and ideas. In the clash of classes, to avoid patronizing poor people and to escape patterns of do-goodism, the religious social worker has a special set of problems.

A muscular young social worker in St. Louis found the youth at the settlement house (under religious sponsorship) hostile and suspicious as he took over his new job. After sizing up the situation, he decided that he had better take on each member of the teenage boxing club there, partly to come to know them, and partly to defend "muscular Christianity." For weeks he sparred with each of the young boxers, and each evening, bruised and at first scarcely able to walk, he got on his bike and rode many blocks to his apartment. The impressed boxers found out that he was also a minister, and marveled. The life of the whole center became more vital, far more people attended the little chapel services, and the whole purpose of the place came into focus.

Only in rare cases would such pugilistic courage (or foolhardiness!) be called for. But the religious social worker must often rely on unorthodox ways to demonstrate the value of religion and his or her commitment to becoming part of the community. Such workers believe that they offer a far fuller message, and deeper effectiveness, if they are known to be religious in their own daily life.

It is important, we are told, that social workers with a religious motivation be all the more confident of their professional qualifications as they take their place among secular colleagues. A tendency to downgrade religious programs is best met by having degrees and experience quite as impressive as those of secular social workers. To attend a recognized graduate school of social work and add that credential to religious motivation and experience is particularly relevant in this occupational field.

This is equally appropriate for the staff member of a congregation who does social work—counseling with families on welfare, providing care for children and youth, and relating to the church or temple with public agencies and programs. Such duties in Catholic parishes also demand expertness and dedication of sisters or others in orders. It's a simple fact that religious social work is a tough job, and that the position will continue to attract only the ablest candidates in the field.

9

EDUCATIONAL BACKGROUND

PEOPLE OF ALL educational backgrounds are represented throughout the religious careers. For example, consider the congregations in hundreds of towns and cities that are often successfully preached to by men and women who never finished high school. And what about the woman with a graduate degree in electrical engineering who takes vows with a Catholic order of sisters and sets off for seminary? Or the junior Phi Beta Kappa in college who stumbles upon early Mennonite history and adopts it as a scholarly career? The Jewish physics instructor who leaves the university to attend theological school for the rabbinate. The math major who barely made it through college yet now teaches computer programming at a mission school in Kenya?

One clue about training for careers in religion echoes the opening paragraphs of this book: to be helpful, you need to summon every available truth and skill. This means mastering deep knowledge and also being fervent and innovative in giving it to others.

Doctors must be experts about the body. Lawyers, engineers, and chemists all must know their specialty in depth. Careers in religion go even further, as they call us to be specialists in the whole person—spirit, mind, and body.

This requires knowledge of psychology, social studies, Scripture interpretation, philosophy, literature, public speaking, music, art, history, child care, the problems of aging—in short, the entire gamut of human life. But how are you to proceed to gain the knowledge and skills required by such a broad endeavor?

High School

At what point in your education do you decide on a religious career? It is essential that you be open-minded, even if you have inwardly concluded that you are called to work in religion. Elsewhere in this book it has been suggested that rather than declaring this call at large, you may do better to grow quietly into it. This prevents a student from being put immediately into a pigeonhole and regarded as "holier than thou," or shaped by others' expectations rather than by God's. It also keeps open a variety of educational pathways.

There is a special skill required by those headed toward a career in religion: proficiency in English. Years ago a survey by the National Education Association revealed the unexpected fact that those students who excel in English often turn out to be good at human relations as well. This is one aspect of the claim that, in high school, the most essential achievement for all students is to learn to communicate. To be successful, students must be able to write a good sentence, spell, know great literature, and grasp the lilt of a poem, the pathos of drama, or the impact of a profound essay.

Communication skills equip us to convey the Word in art, music, and words.

A second type of knowledge to acquire in these years is a sense of history. Since this is the account of how people have reacted to situations, how they have made decisions, and how they dealt with the outcome of their actions, history enables us to participate wisely in the human scenario. There is a familiar quotation to the effect that those who fail to learn the lessons of history are condemned to repeat them. Studying intently the lessons of history in high school is extremely worthwhile if we intend to take part in history ourselves.

To be sure, the high school student considering religion also needs an appreciation of science, mathematics, languages, and the arts. But more urgent than any of these in religious work are English and history. Many years ago, the Association of Theological Schools began to give top priority to these two subjects in listing major fields of preparatory study.

Grades are, of course, a valuable incentive during any period of study. However, when high school is all over, the record that follows each student says little about activities other than academic ones. Your grades, in black-and-white, are an account of how you carried out your vocation as a student. But by no means do grades offer a complete picture of the individual.

Extracurricular activities are also part of the record that one carries away from school. The candidate for a career in religion who has never taken serious part in out-of-class activities is usually held in some suspicion by those judging her or him later on. Participation in athletics, hobby clubs, student government, theater, and music and literary groups all figure in your total personal development.

But, of course, there are those candidates who find that they have little or no interest in such activities; nonetheless, they should not consider themselves unfit for religious service. Although test results tend to show that extroverted, socially involved people are happiest and most successful in religious occupations, there are no hard-and-fast rules on this. Don't try to force an aptitude or inclination if it is not really your own.

Guidance testing is a service provided in most high schools that may be useful in selecting one's occupational field. Basically tests are of three kinds: aptitude tests, interest tests, and psychological tests. Obviously, aptitude measurement seeks to discover one's native gifts: "Am I better at mechanical tasks, mathematics, interpersonal relations, self-expression, or what?" Interest tests try to nail down the field or fields that please or excite the candidate and whether he or she has any aptitude in such matters. The combination of aptitude and interest measurement can show you both what you do well and what you like to do. These two considerations do not always coincide, but having this information earlier on can help you plan your studies wisely.

Beyond these two types of measurement, psychological testing is an index of how steady your personal moods are, how you evaluate yourself as a person, and what your ups and downs of attitude are likely to be. Being introverted, looking within yourself, has advantages in certain job fields. By contrast, being extroverted means you are outward, receptive, and open. Such testing may enable a perceptive counselor to help you with studies and extracurricular activities. Sometimes psychological testing may also indicate your level of interests—whether you care very much about any subject or activity.

It can be valuable for you to have such clues about yourself as you make your way forward in occupational preparation. Be warned, however, that you must neither leap to conclusions because of a test score, nor allow your self-evaluation to be swayed solely by scientific test data. Only a trained guidance adviser should interpret these kinds of test scores.

Home and community activities during high school days can be as revealing and as helpful as studies and extracurricular participation. These are years in which your personal life of prayer may be deeper and more adventurous than at any time during the rest of your life. Reading devotional classics for the first time, sharing ancient and modern prayers, joining with a small circle in group silence or prayers—these are fresh experiences during teen years that can never be known again for the first time. Spiritual friendships among young people can be simpler than ever again. The person thinking of a career in religion is well advised to live as deeply and spontaneously as possible during high school years. Acting in dramatic presentations, singing and playing music, hiking wilderness trails and identifying wildflowers, sitting in awe at sunsets—all these are activities that can be important at this age.

Taking part in the organized program of your church, mosque, or temple is likewise significant. There are a number of worthwhile activities you can engage in, such as teaching a children's class, sharing in a Scout troop, singing in the choir, joining a group traveling to religious assemblies, corresponding with a pen pal in an overseas mission, or making a banner for a festival. In all things, let these so-called formative years shape in you a character and purpose and eagerness that will carry through your whole life.

College or University

How much education is required for careers in religion? Some candidates leave high school, or get only a high school diploma, to enroll in a Bible institute or other specialized religion school. They may have been cautioned that "to go to college will just raise questions you can't ever answer, load you down with subjects you'll never need, and lump you in with a campus swarming with nonbelievers." In the religion school, conversely, there is Scripture study of a practical, ready-to-use kind, with training in preaching and teaching. Worship services are frequent and often mandatory. In some schools there is even a course in "tracting," which is the art of handing leaflets to passersby and getting them to keep them. For some religious ministries, such a course is all that is required for ordination—a sort of trade-school approach to a life's crucial work.

Most leaders of congregations find such purely religious education insufficient. They point out that piety and fervor alone cannot take the place of serious and well-reasoned dealings with the whole mindset of the modern world and its religious heritage. College is the preferred training ground.

Choosing a college or university can be a complicated exercise. Possibly the decision has already been made, based on geography, cost, or family tradition. When choosing a college for religious study, most candidates confer with leaders of their religious group regarding their plans. Is it advantageous, or even required, that they attend a school affiliated with their religion? Is a tax-supported, private, or Ivy League institution preferable? Should parents, who will probably have to bear much of the cost, have an important say in the choice?

The factors involved in choosing a college are many for anyone considering an occupation in religion. Past academic grades may open or close some possibilities. So may tuition costs and other expenses. What are the residence arrangements? What do you judge to be the main concerns of the campus: sports, partying, science, preprofessional preparation, the humanities, religious instruction, music, prestige? How do these emphases coincide with your personal concerns and requirements?

Some advisers suggest that for undergraduate years, a relatively small student body and faculty are preferable; for graduate study, the larger schools are better. Why? On a campus of, say, one thousand students, friendships are more readily made and you can know everyone by sight. Compared with a school of twenty thousand, the smaller school gives you twenty times the chance to be a newspaper editor, leading actress, or some other personality. Such involvement is vital to your personal development; everyone needs to stand out in the crowd in some manner. Later, for graduate work, there is special value for you in the huge library, concerts and athletic facilities, noted professors, and competition of a large university. The more personal and individual your undergraduate situation is, the more useful it may be for preparation in the field of religious leadership.

What major should you choose? Oddly enough, there is wisdom in not taking a lot of religion courses during your undergraduate years. One seminary head insists: "Get culture in college; get theological culture in seminary." He points out that this means not using up valuable time in religion courses, when much of the material learned in these courses must be repeated or repealed when the student gets to seminary. Rather, the candidate (as has been proposed earlier) may well spend college time and effort taking classes in English, history, philosophy, psychology, classics, languages, art, sociology, computer science, and other disciplines that round out the whole personality.

Understandably, college professors of religion mourn such advice: "This takes away our most interested students," they object.

Certainly the idea is not for any dedicated undergraduate to boycott religion courses, but simply to get the most complete education possible.

Innovative Programs

In addition to traditional religious-studies curricula, a number of schools have developed special programs to prepare students for diverse roles in religious areas. For example, at Augustana University College, a Lutheran school located in Alberta, Canada, students may earn a bachelor of arts in religious studies degree with a focus in one of the following three skill areas: Outdoor Ministry, Christian Leadership, or International Development and Christian Formation.

In Outdoor Ministry, students master the use the resources of nature, solitude, and community to enrich other people's religious and spiritual lives. In the process, they develop skills in areas including interpersonal and group relationships, the foundations of religious education, the Christian understanding of nature, experiential education, and physical skills such as canoeing, swimming, and skiing. Courses include the following:

Religious Expression in Drama
Introduction to Educational Psychology: Development
Introduction to Outdoor Pursuits
Cold-Weather Outdoor Pursuits
Warm-Weather Outdoor Pursuits
Arctic Canoe Expedition
Leadership Practicum
Interpersonal and Group Skills Development

Hebrew Prophets
Modern Ethics
Religious Awareness
Topics in Religious Studies (Practicum in Christian
    Ministry)
Topics in Religious Studies (Ecological Theologies)

In the Christian Leadership area, skills are developed in the theory and practice of Christian education, mutual ministry support, worship leadership, spiritual direction, and interpersonal and group interactions. Students take courses such as the following:

Hebrew Prophets
Religious Awareness
Religious Expression in Drama
Study of Classroom Behavior
Introduction to Development Studies
Music Performance (Organ, Voice, Piano, Flute, Guitar,
    Violin, Trumpet)
Introduction to Music
Choir
Introduction to Conducting
Leadership Practicum
Introduction to Educational Psychology: Development
International Development and Christian Formation

In the International Development area, students spend a semester in Mexico or western Ghana (Africa) and a semester in rural Alberta where they engage in volunteer work. They live and interact with host families; undergo intensive language training; develop leadership, communication, and organizational skills; and reflect on relevant spiritual and theological issues pertinent to cross-cultural encounters and international development.

Available courses, in addition to those noted above, include:

Introduction to Development Studies
Development Studies Seminar
Development Studies Practicum
Justice Theologies of the Twentieth Century

Other schools also offer nontraditional programs; check catalogs and program brochures for course listings and descriptions.

Interests outside the curriculum, as in high school, become for many the essence of undergraduate life. The candidate confronts a range of options: sports, chapel choir or band, discussions with guest visitors, art projects, sharing a nearby worship program, summer camp counselor jobs, writing and editing, visiting the town hospital, youth clubs, campus political campaigns, dancing and dating, and a hundred more activities in addition to these.

One added note: the candidate for an occupation in religion does have the responsibility to uphold the traditions of worship and spiritual concern on campus, for one's witness to truth has already begun here. To bypass or avoid a reasonable sharing of religious activity on campus is to let down your fellow students. This doesn't mean adopting a pious and judgmental attitude, but it does mean standing up to be counted when issues arise and sharing buoyantly and frankly in campus religious life.

Again, grades are a consideration. Your academic standing in college can determine the kind of graduate school you will be able to enter, for at this level there is usually real competition. At one seminary, three out of every four applications in most years were rejected on the basis of grades. In college, the candidate's calling is to earn the best academic standing possible to better serve your religion.

Recently, graduate record examinations, which are often routinely required for graduate admissions, showed the academic standing of religion students to be well below all other professional groups—a sorry state of affairs indeed. A longtime professor in a Southern college mused that clergy candidates year after year come from the top tenth and the bottom tenth of college classes, with few between. Top-tenth students were venturesome, solid workers, many of them deciding late upon this field of work; bottom-tenth candidates just got by, had unimpressive personalities in many cases, and had opted for their occupational choice years before. On this basis, it becomes the emphatic purpose of the ordaining authorities to encourage more of the top-tenth students and either to frown upon or to revive those in the bottom tenth.

Seminary

Most readers of this book will probably find the choice of a theological school to be a step pretty far into the future. But at any stage of decision, some light can be shed on the seminary pathway ahead.

At the end of this book you will find a complete list of accredited seminaries. Accreditation involves such factors as size of the library, number of professors employed full-time, and separateness of the campus from any adjoining college. Canadian schools, of which there are a great number of both Protestant and Catholic, are also listed along with those in the United States. Any prospective seminarian may want to contact the schools he or she is interested in for more information, even years in advance.

Theological schools are in the vast majority owned and subsidized by their religious groups to keep pure and lively their beliefs and procedures. So it has become usual that candidates for the priesthood or orders attend college and then a graduate seminary before ordination. Some Protestant denominations similarly require seminary attendance for one year or all three, in a school of their own tradition. Others permit considerable freedom to go to any accredited theological seminary, so long as special courses are provided in the candidate's own tradition. Some theological institutions, in turn, demand denominational approval before they will accept an applicant. Jewish candidates in the Reform group are usually free to select their seminary but must face examinations in their particular group before being ordained.

A new development appeared in the mid-twentieth century, in which a number of seminarians were deliberately offered only one year of study, paid for, with leeway about continuing on for the other two years. It was in effect a trial year to see whether a career in religion was for them. The idea began in 1954 when the Fund for Theological Education, then Rockefeller-endowed, began to appoint some sixty annual Rockefeller Fellows for this one-year experience. A significant requirement of this program was that none of those chosen, by application and interview, had already decided to enter the ministry. A majority of the hundreds of Rockefeller Fellows stayed on to finish seminary, and a great many became notable clergypeople or religion teachers. This program prompted a good number of men and women to sign up for seminary on a one-trial-year basis. Such one-year mobility has meant that more and more students take their first year in one school, then shift to another for their remaining two years, thus getting the expanded breadth of two graduate programs. The program continues on a much smaller scale.

Can you finance a year of study abroad at some accredited theological school where you can speak the language? A first year abroad is the interchangeable one, with basic courses, whereas in the subsequent two years, students specialize and grow widely apart. This splitting of the seminary course naturally meets opposition, as most seminaries would prefer that everyone take the full programs that they offer. But for anyone thinking of a varied, fast-paced three years of theological study, the two-school pattern has a continuing appeal.

Far more women than ever before now take seminary work. This is true not only in Protestant denominations, but also in Catholic schools. A rising, although smaller, number of women is found also in Jewish theological study. Most women, whether their group ordains women or not, follow the same course of study that men take toward ordination.

Field education is a part of every seminary curriculum. It parallels requirements in training for medicine, social work, counseling, law, or teaching by providing actual practice of the ideas and methods introduced in class. For the seminarian, this can often be hospital service on weekends or during summers. An assistantship with a nearby clergyperson is a common assignment. Student chaplain duties at a jail or retirement home also can qualify. Teaching children, serving as the religious reference librarian in the city library, playing the organ at a minority chapel, or organizing a boys' club— each is an example of seminary field education. Reports, supervisors, practicums, and seminars are all common aspects of field education. Sometimes considered a bother, especially to students with exclusively intellectual or abstract interests, a field assignment is also sometimes the one reason some seminarians stay in school at all: it thrusts them daily into flesh-and-blood encounters with actual people. It frequently is also a financial resource, as student budgets suffer especially from inflation and rising prices.

Where can you get the money for seminary? Unless you are affluent, you may well plan to borrow. This calls for many decisions. Is it advisable to earn more and study less, or study more now and pay up after graduation? Depending on individual situations, the only choice here may point toward paying debts during the first, poorly compensated years of a clergy career. "Study now, pay later" is, however, the choice of many theological students. Denominational scholarships are, of course, a backstop.

What degrees are earned in seminary? Most nonsectarian institutions award a master of divinity (M.Div.) after three years of study. The M.Div. is the standard preordination degree. (Until the 1960s, it was called the B.D. or bachelor of divinity; however, many students found it disappointing to get only another bachelor's degree after three years of additional study.) Some schools offer the doctor of ministry (D.Min.), which involves many more years of study after the M.Div. This degree is not an academic achievement like the Ph.D., but a professional degree acknowledging advanced skills in actual clerical tasks. It usually demands some class work during the summers at a seminary, seminar study elsewhere, and a major paper. The doctor of divinity (D.D.) is, of course, merely honorary.

At the same sort of schools, directors of religious education and others may qualify for a master of religious education (M.R.E.). A similar master of arts in religion (M.A.R.) is usually granted only by a university after two years of study. Certain other seminaries offer a doctor of theology (Th.D.) or a master of sacred theology (S.T.M.) for several years of study beyond the M.Div.

In all this preparation for tackling a religious job, the main emphasis is on learning to use resources. This includes knowing how to carry on one's own study of Scripture, where to go in a library or online to get wanted facts, and what storehouses of knowledge and information are available in the crafting of one's ministry. The normal reaction of most people upon seeing a clergyperson's library—far larger than most—is, "Have you really read all these books?" The reply may well be, "No, I haven't. But I know where to find what I want in every one of them when I need it."

This also connotes learning how to keep learning. Many clergy members sign up year after year for continuing education courses. Indeed, the contract arranged with many clergypeople today includes an annual paid study leave that is quite separate from their vacation time.

Spiritual Growth

Spiritual deepening is surely an aspect of preparation for a career in religion. Growth in prayer, intercession for others, and increasing skills in meditating before God are of the essence.

Spiritual maturity in this field is even more mandatory than are knowledge or skills. The candidate for religious work is evaluated instinctively and often publicly. Traits such as phoniness, self-centeredness, tenseness and insecurity, and pettiness in the place of expansiveness and generosity are naturally to be avoided.

How does one gain that aura of being absolutely genuine and real? The faces and demeanor of nuns and monks who have spent thousands of hours kneeling in quiet devotion cannot be counterfeited. Nor can the glow and dynamism of an old Jewish cantor. Or the radiant charm of a lively Methodist missionary. Only the depth of your own spiritual life, achieved through study, meditation, and prayer, can give you this authenticity as you go about your daily chores.

Each person must discover his or her own path toward holiness. In this respect, preparation for a career in religious service demands inward discipline, together with freedom to worship and to communicate religious messages accurately and passionately.

Appendix A

Religion Yearbooks

Anyone seriously interested in a career in religion may well want to buy, or borrow from a library, the most comprehensive annual handbook of information on his or her own tradition.

Catholic

The Catholic Almanac
  Our Sunday Visitor, Inc.
  200 Noll Plaza
  Huntington, IN 46750

  This is an amazing assemblage of statistics, project descriptions, current church news, and lists of bishops and agencies.

Protestant

Yearbook of American and Canadian Churches
Abingdon Press
P.O. Box 801
Nashville, TN 37202-0801

Less encyclopedic than the Catholic book, this annual volume lists denominational figures, bishops, ecumenical organizations, religious periodicals, and service agencies.

Jewish

American Jewish Yearbook
American Jewish Committee
165 E. Fifty-Sixth St.
New York, NY 10022

Dealing with all the American groups in Judaism, this is an authoritative, though not "official," handbook.

Appendix B

Other Sources of Information

THE FOLLOWING LIST of agencies and organizations can provide further information on religious careers and activities.

American Association of Pastoral Counselors
9504A Lee Highway
Fairfax, VA 22031-2303
aapc.org
Supports professional development for clergy interested in counseling and for practicing counselors.

American Friends Service Committee
1501 Cherry St.
Philadelphia, PA 19102
afsc.org
Offers data and some jobs in Quaker world missions.

Association of Theological Schools in the United States and Canada
10 Summit Park Dr.
Pittsburgh, PA 15275-1103
ats.edu
Offers seminary listings and advice about preseminary studies.

Bishops' Committee on Vocations
3211 Fourth St. NE
Washington, DC 20017
Provides information about religious vocations.

B'Nai B'Rith International
2020 K St. NW, 7th Fl.
Washington, DC 20006
bbidirect.org
Distributes the *National Jewish Monthly* and news of the national men's
organization Sons of the Covenant.

Bread for the World
50 F St. NW, Ste. 500
Washington, DC 20001
bread.org
Coordinates world hunger action.

Evangelical Development Ministry
5232 Forest La., #106
Dallas, TX 75244
edmi.org
Encourages development of outreach ministries.

Fellowship of Reconciliation
521 N. Broadway
Nyack, NY 10960
forusa.org
Provides program news of this interfaith pacifist group, which has some twenty-five thousand members.

International Association of Women Ministers
579 Main St.
Stroudsburg, PA 18360
Provides professional and networking opportunities for female clergy.

International Christian Youth Exchange
134 W. Twenty-Sixth St.
New York, NY 10001
Provides details on this youth-exchange program.

National Association of Evangelicals
718 Capitol Square Pl. NW
Washington, DC 20024
nae.net
Provides information on this group, founded in 1942, of three million "Bible-believing Christians."

National Catholic Educational Association
1077 Thirtieth St. NW, Ste. 100
Washington, DC 20007-3852
ncea.org
Provides data on parochial and other Catholic schooling.

National Conference of Christians and Jews (NCCJ)
475 Park Ave., 19th Fl.
New York, NY 10016
nccj.org
Provides statements on this historic interfaith movement.

National Conference of Diocesan Vocation Directors
1021 Sea Mountain Highway, Ste. A-2
North Myrtle Beach, SC 29582
ncdvd.org
Offers information on Catholic parish priesthood.

National Conference on Ministry to the Armed Forces
4141 N. Henderson Rd.
Arlington, VA 22203
ncmaf.org
Supports efforts to provide religion support to men and women serving in the military.

National Cursillo Movement
P.O. Box 210226
Dallas, TX 75211
cursillo.org
Provides information on dynamic Catholic weekends for discipline and
renewal, begun in Spain in 1949.

National Interreligious Service Board for Conscientious
    Objectors/Center on Conscience and War (NISBCO)
1830 Connecticut Ave. NW
Washington, DC 20009
nisbco.org
Provides information about programs relevant to objectors to military
service.

National Religious Broadcasters
9510 Technology Dr.
Manassas, VA 20110
nrb.org
Provides information about this professional group.

Pax Christi
532 W. Eighth St.
Erie, PA 16502
paxchristiusa.org
Explains principles and programs of this (U.S.) ten-thousand-member
Catholic peace movement.

Religious Education Association
c/o Interdenomination Theological Center
700 Martin Luther King Dr., SW
Atlanta, GA 30314
religiouseducation.net
Provides accrediting information on Directors of Religious Education.

Society of Christian Philosophers
Department of Philosophy
Calvin College
Grand Rapids, MI 49546-4388
siu.edu/~scp
Encourages interaction among religious scholars.

Sojourners
2401 Fifteenth St. NW
Washington, DC 20009
sojo.net
Publishes a magazine that details its program of evangelical and liberal
social action.

Southern Christian Leadership Conference
591-A Edgewood Ave.
Atlanta, GA 30312
http://sclcnational.org
Provides updating of the political-religious movement shaped by Martin Luther King, Jr.

World Vision
P.O. Box 9716
Federal Way, WA 98063
worldvision.org
Provides news of a colorful, global "faith" mission.

Young Men's Christian Association
101 N. Wacker Dr.
Chicago, IL 60606
ymca.net
Provides personnel data about local Ys and the national movement.

Young Women's Christian Association
1015 Eighteenth St. NW, Ste. 700
Washington, DC 20036
ywca.org
Provides news of this women's program here and abroad.

Youth for Christ
P.O. Box 228822
Denver, CO 80222
gospelcom.net/yfc
Provides news of its workers and programs.

Appendix C

Accredited Theological Schools in the United States and Canada

FOR MANY READERS of this book, the choice of a postcollege professional school will still be far ahead in the future. But some students at any stage of preparation may want to check out a theological school—Protestant, Catholic, or Jewish—for entrance requirements or selection of courses.

The list of nearly two hundred accredited institutions given here, in general, are those accepted by the Association of Theological Schools in the United States and Canada. Denominations, number of students and faculty, and other descriptive details cannot be given in the limited space of this book. A postcard inquiry may bring you data from any of the schools listed.

Acadia Divinity College
31 Horton St.
Wolfville, Nova Scotia
Canada B4P 2R6
http://ace.acadiau.ca/divcol

Alliance Theological Seminary
350 N. Highland Ave.
Nyack, NY 10960-1416
alliance.edu

American Baptist Seminary of the West
2606 Dwight Way
Berkeley, CA 94704-3029
absw.edu

Anderson University School of Theology
1100 E. Fifth St.
Anderson, IN 46012-3462
anderson.edu/academics/sot/core/index.html

Andover Newton Theological School
210 Herrick Rd.
Newton Centre, MA 02159
ants.edu

Aquinas Institute of Theology
3642 Lindell Blvd.
St. Louis, MO 63108-3396
ai.edu

Asbury Theological Seminary
204 N. Lexington Ave.
Wilmore, KY 40390
ats.wilmore.ky.us

Assemblies of God Theological Seminary
1435 N. Glenstone
Springfield, MO 65802
agts.edu

Associated Mennonite Biblical Seminary
3003 Benham Ave.
Elkhart, IN 46517-1999
ambs.edu

Athenaeum of Ohio
6616 Beechmont Ave.
Cincinnati, OH 45230-2091
mtsm.org

Atlantic School of Theology
640 Francklyn St.
Halifax, Nova Scotia
Canada B3H 3B5
http://astheology.ns.ca

Austin Presbyterian Theological Seminary
100 E. Twenty-Seventh St.
Austin, TX 78705-5797
austinseminary.edu

Bangor Theological Seminary
300 Union St.
Bangor, ME 04401
bts.edu

Beeson Divinity School of Samford University
800 Lakeshore Dr.
Birmingham, AL 35229
http://beeson.samford.edu

Berkeley Divinity School
Yale University
363 Saint Roman St.
New Haven, CT 06511
yale.edu/divinity/bds

Bethany Theological Seminary
615 National Road West
Richmond, IN 47374
brethren.org/bethany

Bethel Theological Seminary
3949 Bethel Dr.
St. Paul, MN 55112

Bexley Hall
1100 S. Goodman St.
Rochester, NY 14620
http://bexley.edu.anglican.org

Biblical Theological Seminary
200 N. Main St.
Hatfield, PA 19440
biblical.edu

Boston University School of Theology
745 Commonwealth Ave.
Boston, MA 02115
bu.edu/sth

Brite Divinity School
Texas Christian University
TCU Box 298130
2800 S. University Dr.
Fort Worth, TX 76129
brite.tcu.edu/brite

Calvin Theological Seminary
3233 Burton St. SE
Grand Rapids, MI 49546
calvinseminary.edu

Canadian Theological Seminary
4400 Fourth Ave.
Regina, Saskatchewan
Canada S4T 0H8
cbccts.ca

Candler School of Theology of Emory University
500 Kilgo Circle NE
Atlanta, GA 30322
http://candler.emory.edu

Catholic Theological Union
5401 S. Cornell Ave.
Chicago, IL 60615-5698
ctu.edu

Catholic University of America
Department of Theology
620 Michigan Ave. NE
Washington, DC 20064
http://religiousstudies.cua.edu

Central Baptist Theological Seminary
741 N. Thirty-First St.
Kansas City, KS 66102-3964
cbts.edu

Chicago Theological Seminary
5757 S. University Ave.
Chicago, IL 60637
chgosem.edu

Christ the King Seminary
711 Knox Rd.
P.O. Box 607
East Aurora, NY 14052-0607
cks.edu

Christian Theological Seminary
1000 W. Forty-Second St.
P.O. Box 88267
Indianapolis, IN 46208-3301
cts.edu

Church Divinity School of the Pacific
2451 Ridge Rd.
Berkeley, CA 94709
http://cdsp.edu

Church of God School of Theology
P.O. Box 3330
Cleveland, TN 37320-3330

Claremont School of Theology
1325 N. College Ave.
Claremont, CA 91711-3199
cst.edu

Columbia Biblical Seminary
P.O. Box 3122
Columbia, SC 29230
ciu.edu

Columbia Theological Seminary
701 Columbia Dr.
Decatur, GA 30031
ctsnet.edu

Concordia Seminary
801 DeMun Ave.
St. Louis, MO 63105
csl.edu

Concordia Theological Seminary
6600 N. Clinton St.
Fort Wayne, IN 46825-4996
ctsfw.edu

Covenant Theological Seminary
12330 Conway Rd.
St. Louis, MO 63141
covenantseminary.edu

Dallas Theological Seminary
3909 Swiss Ave.
Dallas, TX 75204
dts.edu

De Sales School of Theology
721 Lawrence St. NE
Washington, DC 20017

Denver (Conservative Baptist) Seminary
P.O. Box 100,000
Denver, CO 80250-0100
denverseminary.edu

Dominican House of Studies
487 Michigan Ave. NE
Washington, DC 20017
dhs.edu

Dominican School of Philosophy and Theology
2401 Ridge Rd.
Berkeley, CA 94709
dspt.edu

Drew University Theological School
36 Madison Ave.
Madison, NJ 07940
drew.edu/theo

Duke University Divinity School
Chapel Dr.
Box 90968
Durham, NC 27708-0968
divinity.duke.edu

Earlham School of Religion
Earlham College
228 College Ave.
Richmond, IN 47374
http://esr.earlham.edu

Eastern Baptist Theological Seminary
6 Lancaster Ave.
Wynnewood, PA 19096-3494

Eastern Mennonite Seminary of Eastern Mennonite University
1200 Park Rd.
Harrisonburg, VA 22801-2462
emu.edu

Eden Theological Seminary
475 E. Lockwood Ave.
St. Louis, MO 63119-3192
eden.edu

Emmanuel College of Victoria University
75 Queen's Park Crescent, East
Toronto, Ontario
Canada M5S 1K7
http://vicu.utoronto.ca/emmanuel/index.htm

Emmanuel School of Religion
One Walker Dr.
Johnson City, TN 37601
esr.edu

Episcopal Divinity School
99 Brattle St.
Cambridge, MA 02138
episdivschool.edu

Episcopal Theological Seminary of the Southwest
606 Rathervue Pl.
P.O. Box 2247
Austin, TX 78768-2247
etss.edu

Erskine Theological Seminary
Drawer 668
Main St.
Due West, SC 29639
erskine.edu/seminary

Evangelical School of Theology
121 S. College St.
Myerstown, PA 17067
evangelical.edu

Evangelical Seminary of Puerto Rico
Ponce de Leon Ave. 776
San Juan, PR 00925
http://netministries.org/see/charmin/cm01399

Franciscan School of Theology
1712 Euclid Ave.
Berkeley, CA 94709
fst.edu

Fuller Theological Seminary
135 N. Oakland Ave.
Pasadena, CA 91182
fuller.edu

Garrett-Evangelical Theological Seminary
2121 Sheridan Rd.
Evanston, IL 60201
garrett.nwu.edu

General Theological Seminary
175 Ninth Ave.
New York, NY 10011-4977
gts.edu

Golden Gate Baptist Theological Seminary
201 Seminary Dr.
Mill Valley, CA 94941-3197
ggbts.edu

Gordon-Conwell Theological Seminary
130 Essex St.
South Hamilton, MA 01982
gordonconwell.edu

Graduate Theological Union
2400 Ridge Rd.
Berkeley, CA 94709
gtu.edu

Haggard Graduate School of Theology of Azusa Pacific University
901 E. Alosta
P.O. Box 7000
Azusa, CA 91702-7000
apu.edu/theology

Hartford Seminary
77 Sherman St.
Hartford, CT 06105
hartsem.edu

Harvard University Divinity School
45 Francis Ave.
Cambridge, MA 02138
hds.harvard.edu

Holy Cross Greek Orthodox School of Theology
50 Goddard Ave.
Brookline, MA 02146
hchc.edu

Howard University School of Divinity
1400 Shepherd St. NE
Washington, DC 20017
washtheocon.org/html/howard.html

Huron College Faculty of Theology
1349 Western Rd.
London, Ontario
Canada N6G 1H3
huronuc.on.ca/theology

Iliff School of Theology
2201 S. University Blvd.
Denver, CO 80210
iliff.edu

Immaculate Conception Seminary
Seton Hall University
400 S. Orange Ave.
South Orange, NJ 07079
http://theology.shu.edu

Interdenominational Theological Center
700 Martin Luther King, Jr., Dr. SW
Atlanta, GA 30314
itc.edu

International School of Theology
24600 Arrowhead Springs Rd.
San Bernardino, CA 92414-0001
leaderu.com/isot

Jesuit School of Theology at Berkeley
1735 LeRoy Ave.
Berkeley, CA 94709-1193
jstb.edu

Joint Board of Theological Colleges
3473 University St.
Montreal, Quebec
Canada H3A 2A8
ww2.mcgill.ca/religion/jbtc.htm

Kenrick-Glennon Seminary
5200 Glennon Dr.
St. Louis, MO 63119-4399
kenrickparish.com

Knox College
59 Saint George St.
Toronto, Ontario
Canada M5S 2E6
utoronto.ca/knox

Lancaster Theological Seminary
555 W. James St.
Lancaster, PA 17603-2897
lts.org

Lexington Theological Seminary
631 S. Limestone St.
Lexington, KY 40508
lextheo.edu

Lincoln Christian College and Seminary
100 Campus View Dr.
Lincoln, IL 62656
lccs.edu

Louisville Presbyterian Theological Seminary
1044 Alta Vista Rd.
Louisville, KY 40205
lpts.edu

Luther Seminary
2481 Como Ave.
St. Paul, MN 55108
luthersem.edu

Lutheran School of Theology at Chicago
1100 E. Fifty-Fifth St.
Chicago, IL 60615-5199
lstc.edu

Lutheran Theological Seminary
114 Seminary Crescent
Saskatoon, Saskatchewan
Canada S7N 0X3
usask.ca/stu/luther

Lutheran Theological Seminary at Gettysburg
61 Seminary Ridge
Gettysburg, PA 17325-1795
ltsg.edu/sem

Lutheran Theological Seminary at Philadelphia
7301 Germantown Ave.
Philadelphia, PA 19119
ltsp.edu

Lutheran Theological Southern Seminary
4201 N. Main St.
Columbia, SC 29203
ltss.edu

McCormick Theological Seminary
5460 S. University Ave.
Chicago, IL 60615
mccormick.edu

McGill University Faculty of Religious Studies
3520 University St.
Montreal, Quebec
Canada H3A 2A7
ww2.mcgill.ca/religion

McMaster Divinity College
Hamilton, Ontario
Canada L8S 4K1
http://divinity.mcmaster.ca/about

Meadville/Lombard Theological School
5701 S. Woodlawn Ave.
Chicago, IL 60637
meadville.edu

Memphis Theological Seminary
168 E. Parkway South at Union
Memphis, TN 38104-4395
mtscampus.edu

Mennonite Brethren Biblical Seminary
4824 E. Butler Ave.
Fresno, CA 93727-5097
mbseminary.com

Methodist Theological School in Ohio
3081 Columbus Pike
Delaware, OH 43015-0931
mtso.edu

Midwestern Baptist Theological Seminary
5001 N. Oak Trafficway
Kansas City, MO 64118
mbts.edu

Moravian Theological Seminary
1200 Main St.
Bethlehem, PA 18018-6650
moravianseminary.edu

Mount Angel Seminary
One Abbey Dr.
St. Benedict, OR 97373
mtangel.edu

Mount Saint Mary's College and Seminary
16300 Old Emmitsburg Rd.
Emmitsburg, MD 21727-7797
msmary.edu/seminary

Multnomah Biblical Seminary
8435 NE Glisan St.
Portland, OR 97220
multnomah.edu

Nashotah House
2777 Mission Rd.
Nashotah, WI 53058-9793
nashotah.edu

Nazarene Theological Seminary
1700 E. Meyer Blvd.
Kansas City, MO 64131
nts.edu

New Brunswick Theological Seminary
17 Seminary Pl.
New Brunswick, NJ 08901-1196
nbts.edu

New Orleans Baptist Theological Seminary
3939 Gentilly Blvd.
New Orleans, LA 70126-4858
nobts.edu

New York Theological Seminary
475 Riverside Dr.
New York, NY 10115
nyts.edu/enter.htm

Newman Theological College
15611 St. Albert Trail
Edmonton, Alberta
Canada T5L 4H8
newman.edu

North American Baptist Seminary
1525 S. Grange Ave.
Sioux Falls, SD 57105-1599
nabs.edu

North Park Theological Seminary
3225 W. Foster Ave.
Chicago, IL 60625-4895
northpark.edu/sem

Northern Baptist Theological Seminary
660 E. Butterfield Rd.
Lombard, IL 60148
seminary.edu

Notre Dame Seminary
2901 S. Carrollton Ave.
New Orleans, LA 70118-4391
nds.edu

Oblate College
391 Michigan Ave. NE
Washington, DC 20017

Oblate School of Theology
285 Oblate Dr.
San Antonio, TX 78216-6693
ost.edu

Ontario Theological Seminary
25 Ballyconnor Court
North York, Ontario
Canada M2M 4B3

Oral Roberts University School of Theology
7777 S. Lewis Ave.
Tulsa, OK 74171
oru.edu

Pacific Lutheran Theological Seminary
2770 Marin Ave.
Berkeley, CA 94708-1597
plts.edu

Pacific School of Religion
1798 Scenic Ave.
Berkeley, CA 94709
psr.edu

Payne Theological Seminary
1230 Wilberforce Clifton Rd.
Wilberforce, OH 45384
payne.edu

Perkins School of Theology
Southern Methodist University
5915 Bishop Blvd.
P.O. Box 750133
Dallas, TX 75275-0133
smu.edu/theology

Phillips Theological Seminary
901 N. Mingo Rd.
Tulsa, OK 74116
ptstulsa.edu

Pittsburgh Theological Seminary
616 N. Highland Ave.
Pittsburgh, PA 15206
pts.edu

Pontifical College Josephinum
7625 N. High St.
Columbus, OH 43235
pcj.edu

Pope John XXIII National Seminary
558 South Ave.
Weston, MA 02193-2699
geocities.com/bjxxiii

Presbyterian School of Christian Education
3401 Brook Rd.
Richmond, VA 23227
union-psce.edu

Princeton Theological Seminary
64 Mercer St.
P.O. Box 821
Princeton, NJ 08542-0803
ptsem.edu

Protestant Episcopal Theological Seminary in Virginia
3737 Seminary Rd.
Alexandria, VA 22304
vts.edu

Providence College and Seminary
General Delivery
Otterburne, Manitoba
Canada R0A 1G0
http://prov.ca

Queen's Theological College
Rm. 212, Theological Hall
Kingston, Ontario
Canada K7L 3N6
queensu.ca/theology

Reformed Presbyterian Theological Seminary
7418 Penn Ave.
Pittsburgh, PA 15208
rpts.edu

Reformed Theological Seminary
5422 Clinton Blvd.
Jackson, MS 39209
rts.edu

Regent College
5800 University Blvd.
Vancouver, British Columbia
Canada V6T 2E4
gospelcom.net/regent/regentnew

Regent University School of Divinity
1000 Regent University Dr.
Virginia Beach, VA 23464-9870
regent.edu/acad/schdiv

Regis College
15 St. Mary St.
Toronto, Ontario
Canada M4Y 2R5
utoronto.ca/regis

Sacred Heart Major Seminary
2701 Chicago Blvd.
Detroit, MI 48206
aodonline.org/shms/shms.htm

Sacred Heart School of Theology
7335 S. Highway 100
P.O. Box 429
Hales Corners, WI 53130-0429
shst.edu

St. Andrew's College
1121 College Dr.
Saskatoon, Saskatchewan
Canada S7N 0W3
ualberta.ca/st.stephens/sa-home.htm

St. Augustine's Seminary of Toronto
2661 Kingston Rd.
Scarborough, Ontario
Canada M1M 1M3
staugustines.on.ca

St. Bernard's Institute
1100 S. Goodman St.
Rochester, NY 14620
stbernards.edu

St. Charles Borromeo Seminary
Overbrook
1000 E. Wynnewood Rd.
Wynnewood, PA 19096-3002
scs.edu

Saint Francis Seminary
3257 S. Lake Dr.
St. Francis, WI 53235
sfs.edu

St. John's Seminary
5012 Seminary Rd.
Camarillo, CA 93012-2598
sjsc.edu

St. John's Seminary
127 Lake St.
Brighton, MA 02135
sjs.edu

St. John's University School of Theology
P.O. Box 7288
Luke Hall 201
Collegeville, MN 56321
csbsju.edu/sot/index.html

St. Joseph's Seminary
201 Seminary Ave. (Dunwoodie)
Yonkers, NY 10704

Saint Mary Seminary
28700 Euclid Ave.
Wyckliffe, OH 44092-2585
stmarysem.edu

St. Mary's Seminary and University
5400 Roland Ave.
Baltimore, MD 21210
stmarys.edu

St. Meinrad School of Theology
200 Hill Dr.
St. Meinrad, IN 47577
saintmeinrad.edu/theology

St. Patrick's Seminary
320 Middlefield Rd.
Menlo Park, CA 94025
stpatricksseminary.org

Saint Paul School of Theology
5123 Truman Rd.
Kansas City, MO 64127
spst.edu

Saint Paul Seminary School of Divinity of the University of
St. Thomas
2260 Summit Ave.
St. Paul, MN 55105
stthomas.edu

St. Peter's Seminary
1040 Waterloo St. North
London, Ontario
Canada N6A 3Y1
rcec.london.on.ca/seminary.htm

St. Vincent De Paul Regional Seminary
10701 S. Military Trail
Boynton Beach, FL 33436-4811
http://svdp.edu

Saint Vincent Seminary
300 Fraser Purchase Rd.
Latrobe, PA 15650-2690
http://benedictine.stvincent.edu/seminary/mainpage.html

St. Vladimir's Orthodox Theological Seminary
575 Scarsdale Rd.
Crestwood, NY 10707
svots.edu

SS. Cyril and Methodius Seminary
3535 Indian Trail
Orchard Lake, MI 48324
http://orchardlakeseminary.org/form.html

San Francisco Theological Seminary
2 Kensington Rd.
San Anselmo, CA 94960
sfts.edu

Seabury-Western Theological Seminary
2122 Sheridan Rd.
Evanston, IL 60201-2938
seabury.edu

Seattle University School of Theology and Ministry
900 Broadway
Seattle, WA 98122
seattleu.edu/theomin

Seminary of the Immaculate Conception
440 W. Neck Rd.
Huntington, NY 11743
icseminary.edu

Seventh-Day Adventist Theological Seminary of Andrews
   University
Andrews University
Berrien Springs, MI 49104-1500
andrews.edu/sem

Southeastern Baptist Theological Seminary
222 N. Wingate
P.O. Box 1889
Wake Forest, NC 27588-1889
sebts.edu

Southern Baptist Theological Seminary
2825 Lexington Rd.
Louisville, KY 40280
sbts.edu

Southwestern Baptist Theological Seminary
P.O. Box 22000
Fort Worth, TX 76122
swbts.edu

Staff King School for the Ministry
2441 LeConte Ave.
Berkeley, CA 94709

Talbot School of Theology of Biola University
13800 Biola Ave.
La Mirada, CA 90639
talbot.edu

Toronto School of Theology
47 Queens Park Crescent East
Toronto, Ontario
Canada M5S 2C3
tst.edu

Trinity College Faculty of Divinity
6 Hoskin Ave.
Toronto, Ontario
Canada M5S 1H8
trinity.utoronto.ca/divinity

Trinity Episcopal School for Ministry
311 Eleventh St.
Ambridge, PA 15003
tesm.edu

Trinity Evangelical Divinity School of Trinity International
   University
2065 Half Day Rd.
Deerfield, IL 60015
tiu.edu

Trinity Lutheran Seminary
2199 E. Main St.
Columbus, OH 43209-2334
trinity.capital.edu

Union Theological Seminary
3041 Broadway
New York, NY 10027-0003
uts.columbia.edu

Union Theological Seminary in Virginia
3401 Brook Rd.
Richmond, VA 23227

United Theological Seminary
1810 Harvard Blvd.
Dayton, OH 45406
united.edu

United Theological Seminary of the Twin Cities
3000 Fifth St. NW
New Brighton, MN 55112
unitedseminary-mn.org

University of Chicago Divinity School
Swift Hall
1025 E. Fifty-Eighth St.
Chicago, IL 60637
http://divinity.uchicago.edu

University of Dubuque Theological Seminary
2000 University Ave.
Dubuque, IA 52001
http://udts.dbq.edu

University of Notre Dame Department of Theology
130 Malloy Hall
Notre Dame, IN 46556
nd.edu/~theo

University of St. Mary of the Lake Mundelein Seminary
1000 E. Maple Ave.
Mundelein, IL 60060
vocations.org

University of St. Michael's College Faculty of Theology
81 St. Mary St.
Toronto, Ontario
Canada M5S 1J4
utoronto.ca/stmikes

University of St. Thomas School of Theology
9845 Memorial Dr.
Houston, TX 77024
stthom.edu

University of the South School of Theology
335 Tennessee Ave.
Sewanee, TN 37383-0001
sewanee.edu

Vancouver School of Theology
6000 Iona Dr.
Vancouver, British Columbia
Canada V6T 1L4
vst.edu

Vanderbilt University Divinity School
411 Twenty-First Ave. South
Nashville, TN 37240
http://divinity.library.vanderbilt.edu/div/index.html

Virginia Union University School of Theology
1500 N. Lombardy St.
Richmond, VA 23220
vuu.edu/theology/home.htm

Wartburg Theological Seminary
333 Wartburg Pl.
Dubuque, IA 52003-7797
wartburgseminary.edu

Washington Theological Union
6896 Laurel St. NW
Washington, DC 20012-2016
wtu.edu

Waterloo Lutheran Seminary
75 University Ave. West
Waterloo, Ontario
Canada N2L 3C5
wlu.ca/~wwwsem/index.shtml

Wesley Biblical Seminary
P.O. Box 9938
Jackson, MS 39286-0938
wbs.edu

Wesley Theological Seminary
4500 Massachusetts Ave. NW
Washington, DC 20016
wesleysem.edu

Western Evangelical Seminary
P.O. Box 23939
Portland, OR 97281

Western Theological Seminary
101 E. Thirteenth St.
Holland, MI 49423
westernsem.org

Westminster Theological Seminary
P.O. Box 27009
Philadelphia, PA 19118
wts.edu

Weston Jesuit School of Theology
3 Phillips Pl.
Cambridge, MA 02138-3495
wjst.edu

Winebrenner Theological Seminary
701 E. Melrose Ave.
P.O. Box 478
Findlay, OH 45839
winebrenner.edu/home.asp

Wycliffe College
5 Hoskin Ave.
Toronto, Ontario
Canada M5S 1H7
utoronto.ca/wycliffe

Yale University Divinity School
409 Prospect St.
New Haven, CT 06510-2167
yale.edu/divinity

About the Author

Pastor, professor, counselor, retreat leader, writer and editor, director at hundreds of youth and student conferences, John Oliver Nelson had an exciting career of his own in religious service. He taught for years at Yale University's graduate divinity school in the field of vocation and served as an adjunct at Drew University and the Earlham School of Religion. He wrote dozens of booklets, books, and vocational study guides.

Dr. Nelson was long the editor of *Intercollegian*, the widely read YMCA–YWCA campus magazine. He set up the vocations program of the national Presbyterian church. Heading the Commission on the Ministry of what is now the National Council of Churches, Dr. Nelson correlated the vocations programs of the many denominations (forty-five million Americans) associated with the National Council of Churches. Later, he served as chairman of the council's department of evangelism for several years; he also served as chairman of the national council of the Fellowship of Reconciliation. Internationally, Dr. Nelson headed the World

Council of Churches' study commission in the United States on the meaning of work and vocation.

Before all this, he had done his college work at Princeton with high honors, a degree at Edinburgh University (Scotland) and McCormick Seminary (Chicago), a Ph.D. at Yale, and a five-year pastorate in Pittsburgh. He founded Kirkridge, a four-hundred-acre ecumenical retreat/conference center on the Appalachian Trail in eastern Pennsylvania where he lived. His wife had a special concern for vocation and was ordained by the United Church of Canada. A son lives in Hawaii. Dr. Nelson's side interests were the viola, Celtic art, calligraphy, programs of alcohol and drug rehabilitation, and prison reform. For this book, he was in active consultation with Jesuit and rabbinical leaders.

Mark Rowh, a professional author of career guidance materials, revised Dr. Nelson's work to create the 2004 edition.